Writing Erotica for

Revised Edition 2022

B.B. Pierce

DEDICATION

"A dirty mind is a terrible thing to waste."
Especially yours.

This erotica eBook/Book is dedicated to all my loyal erotica readers. I ask that once you have finished this eBook/Book, that you take the time to review/rate it for me. Those of you who may be reluctant to use your real names, then just email or dm me your review and I will use it "anonymously". So, this way you can review, yet not reveal your real name. I use them on social media, in my website, and often in future erotica eBooks/Books. If you like I can use the state or country that you reside in, this is completely your choice.

Email bbpierceauthor@yahoo.com or DM me.

Read erotica responsibly and stay safe.

Always stay hydrated while reading erotica in the event of loss of bodily fluids.

Copyright & Disclaimer

---

1. http://canva.com

2. http://pixabay.com

Foreword

I feel I must warn you that since this revised edition is updated from the years ago that the original was written. Therefore, I suggest most of you begin reading this publication from the halfway point.

I mention this because not all of you may be computer users and still enjoy putting pen to paper or use a word processor or even a typewriter to create your stories. If so than much of the first half of this publication is here, just for you to gain more knowledge from. Unfortunately, many of the old school publishers' addresses might no longer be reliable as may be many of the older websites. It does show you the process of using paper and envelope along with keeping track of what you are submitting.

You might have to do your due diligence to research newer publishing houses. There is something out there for everyone. It does show you that writing erotica today and getting it published is much easier than it was years ago. So, you are at an advantage before you even start.

Writing this revision, I wanted to accomplish two things. One to offer the old school material for anyone who wanted to use it and to show just how much work went into erotica writing years ago prior to the internet. Two I wanted to update as much material as possible to again offer guidance to newbie erotica writers in today's marketplace. So hopefully readers can understand where I was coming from, and that each half of this book has valuable information.

This publication offers you 300 FREE erotica story ideas so that you can begin writing immediately. I am here for you 24/7 to answer any questions and willing to review your first story draft for you. Simply contact me anytime.

So now sit back and enjoy the read. I also urge you to read informative writing books of all kinds to absorb as much useful information as possible. Education is something no one can take away from you.

Writing Erotica for Fun & Profit Revised Edition

Chapter 1

Stationary, Letterheads, & Envelopes

Previously upon inquiring about and ordering the course, when it was offered in text format, many of you submitted your requests handwritten, in various sized envelopes with numerous amounts of postage attached. Granted, the requests from Canada, Mexico, and other foreign countries are required to have specific envelopes and postage, but in the United States, we as writers, should adhere to a more formal degree of format.

Stationary should be number 20-pound bond and plain white, letter size. You may have personalized letterheads, complete with logo if you wish. This depends on how much you want to spend. Various full and self-serve printers, plus discount office supply stores can assist you with this. Ask them to show you specific weights, and sizes. Perhaps you may be able to design your own.

The example in this book shows how to make your own letterhead with the help of a typewriter, or word processor, and printer. This, plus a small amount of cutting and pasting, will allow you to create your own design. Then just take it to the printer and make all the copies you need. This format will also serve to assist you as a template for having number 10 size envelopes printed with your logo. A number 10 envelope is approximately 4 1/8" x 9 1/2" in size and can be either 20 or 24 pounds. Personalized letterheads need only be used for query letters, cover letters, and the first page in a manuscript. This will be covered later in the course. Each additional page only needs to have your name, and the title of the story printed at the upper left-hand side. This can save you money on printed stationary.

There are mainly two types of envelopes you will be dealing with in your correspondence exchange with publishing houses. The first, is the everyday number 10 plain white envelope mentioned previously.

This is used primarily for query letters and submitting shorter length, manuscript letters. Always remember to include a Self-Addressed Stamped Envelope (SASE) with all your submissions, and queries. This is another professional courtesy to your editor. It allows them to accept, or reject your work, and notify you accordingly, by sending back either an acceptance form letter, or your original work with a rejection form.

The second envelope is a 9" x 12" or larger, which is used to send lengthier manuscripts. You might investigate the cost of United States Post Office Priority mail rates. They supply you with an envelope as well, which guarantees speedier delivery, but costs slightly more in postage fees. If you want to send many manuscripts in a short time, that may be the way to go, especially Flat Rate Envelopes. Also be sure to include a SASE inside, which can be a #10 envelope. I cannot stress this fact enough. It shows professionalism, and will make you stand out from those, would be professional writers, who do not include a SASE.

Envelopes may have a stamp or gummed label printed return address on them if they do not have a logo. You may also use larger return address labels for larger envelopes. The bottom line is this, do not spend any more money than you must, but do always present a professional appearance in your work.

You might have to make a few trips to the Post Office to weigh your envelopes, just to make certain that you affix the proper amount of postage. This is important, because otherwise your envelopes may not be delivered or worse yet, not be accepted for the reason of postage due. Office supply stores have smaller versions of postage scales, which make it easier to weigh your envelopes at home, and affix postage yourself. Just be certain that the latest postage rates come with the scale. However, if you want to keep expenses down, use the scale at the Post Office, it is FREE.

Many writers include a thin piece of cardboard to help prevent their manuscripts from bending in the mail delivery process. This of course is optional but does show a professional concern from the writer. Manuscripts can be stapled or loose. Just be certain that each page includes the author's name, story title, and page number for continuity. This helps if the pages are ever rearranged.

Many cities now have discount warehouse operations, with merchandise covering all sorts of products. Many of these contain office supply sections, and their prices are extremely competitive. If you belong to one of these outlets in your area, I suggest you compare prices on various sized envelopes, as well as other office supplies you might need to assist you in your writing. Always remember, it is important to not only be professional in your writing, however, also to keep costs down as much as possible. Less cost means greater profits.

Although ultimately it is the content of your written work that the editors will be most concerned with, you might also consider creating a specific look for your submission packages. You might wish to attempt this once you have begun making money with your writing. For instance, you might send your work in a colored envelope, which attracts the editor's immediate attention, therefore being opened prior to others. A distinctive logo, or label is another way of gaining attention.

Please bear in mind, these are costly, and will dip into your profits, so you must be financially ready. In just starting out, you may want to keep your operation simple, and gradually upgrade when you are ready. I often purchase my materials in bulk when I see a good sale going on. This way I save money, and the supplies last me awhile, so that I can spend more time writing, and less time shopping for supplies.

For those of you who have downloaded this book on the Internet, you already know how easy it is to use your computer and sell your work to an e-book publisher. Once again you can see how this is yet another way to sell your erotica writing. However, your writing supplies will be a computer, and an Internet service provider. Again, I suggest you shop around for costs.

Chapter 2

Handwritten Versus Typed

All forms of correspondence, and manuscript submissions should be typed or printed. Now if you are only able to produce handwritten stories currently, relax. There are several solutions. First you may find a friend of legal age, who will type them for you, or you can enlist the aid of a professional typing service. However, you should first warn them about the type of material it is you wish duplicated, in the event they may disapprove of such literature.

Remember, those self-service printers mentioned earlier? Most of them have typewriters, and word processors you can rent time on. You may have to resort to these methods, until you have money to invest in your own equipment. The best way to look for low-cost machinery is in the classified section of the newspaper, and you can place an ad for what it is you want. Pawn or thrift shops usually have a selection of typewriters, word processors, computers, and printers. With the computer industry changing so rapidly there are always good deals around.

You just need a word processing software program, and a good printer. So, ask around, and put the word out for what you are looking for. Believe me, I am far from a typing, or computer whiz, but the editors do not know this. Using a word processor/computer is just like typing, use the hunt and peck method, I do. There are some fantastic software publishing/word processing programs out there. Even now, some manufacturers have software, which allows you to dictate your story, and the computer types it for you.

Many of these software programs will check your copy/text for spelling, and grammar mistakes, plus include a thesaurus. You can store all your work on disks, thumb drives, or hard drive, and have it printed up later. Many editors are now giving the option of submitting work on computer disks, and electronic mail (E-mail). You might have to inquire if they also desire hard copy to be sent along with the computer disk. This course was on 3.5" computer disk, so you can see just how versatile it is.

This is a personal decision, as only you know what will be best suitable to your writing needs. The good point is that these are all tools, and part of certain business expenses you will incur as a writer. Be aware that good buys are out there, especially when new items are introduced, and the retailers are having sales on the discontinued models. Ask others for a referral on products that they use.

Concerning type/fonts, this is entirely up to you, and your editors. They will be the ones who dictate the final font, if you submit your work in one, they disagree with. You won't go wrong by using the fonts you see in most books that have already been published. There is nothing wrong with creativity, just if the editor approves. This font is Times New Roman, with type size 14.

Chapter 3

Query Letters

Now that you know the proper type of stationery and envelopes to use, let's learn about query letters. A query letter is just what it seems, a letter asking a particular question. In our case they are continually used. There is an example of one in the Lists & Logs section at the end of this course.

First, we need to send one to every new publishing house we find, asking for a set of their Writer's Guidelines. Whenever sending a query letter, or manuscript submission, be sure to include a SASE. I cannot emphasize this fact enough. Usually, I write the name of the publisher under my return address so that I can identify the SASE immediately when it returns. This not only shows you are a professional, but also insures a speedier response to your questions. In the event it is a manuscript submission, the editor will most likely send you either an acceptance, or a rejection letter inside. Be advised that many of these are form letters. In the event they wish to correspond with you, they may also use the SASE. Accept the fact that the more professional your work appears, the more professionally it will be received.

If you have not already, then you are now becoming a writer. When you receive payment for writing services, you are then a professional writer. Once we know the guidelines, and have submitted our work, we may want to send a query letter, as to the progress of our work. This also keeps a direct line of communication between you, and the editors, keeping your name in front of them. The fine line you must keep, is not to be too bothersome. Most editors are extremely busy.

Online you can request Writer's Guidelines via email. Many websites of erotica publishers have a section, which includes the Writer Guidelines they adhere to, and you can always print these out, or store them on your hard drive.

You can also use email to contact publishers, and your editors.

Chapter 4

Writer's Guidelines

Writer's Guidelines are what that publisher expects you, as a writer, to adhere too. They will usually spell out what types of stories the editor wants, how to submit them, and in what quantities, payment rates, and guidelines. Often, they will inform you how to obtain a copy of their work, so you will be able to research them more thoroughly. We'll touch upon this later in the course.

Once you obtain the necessary guidelines, and have finished your manuscripts, it is time to submit them. Again remember, keep professional quality about your work. One thing not to do is make numerous submissions. This means, do not send the same stories to different publishers, or they will only return them to you, unread. You might think, "How will they know I have sent out numerous submissions?" That is not the problem. The problem arises when you suddenly receive acceptance letters from two different publishers for the same story. No matter what steps you take attempting to remedy the problem, you have already lost much of your credibility with both editors, and they will be wary accepting any more of your work. So be patient, submit only one story at a time. The best way to achieve this is by keeping careful records, and to be consistent.

As one publisher returns a story, you have two choices. If it needs rewriting do so and resubmit it too the same publisher stating so. If it is rejected for subject matter, or length being inappropriate for that publisher, then you can resubmit it to another, unchanged. Since Writer's Guidelines are what that publisher expects, you must follow them very carefully. Every publisher is different, and many must answer to different censors. They will usually spell out precisely what types of stories they are able to accept. What is taboo to one may be highly acceptable to another. As I mentioned previously, always stay legal in your writing.

Some publishers only want shorter stories and are very explicit about the length you should submit, as well as the number of manuscripts sent in at one time. These are called simultaneous submissions, not to be confused with numerous submissions. When that happens to me, I merely divide my excessive number of stories into smaller amounts, then send them in every few weeks, or once a month, until the editor has all of them. Again remember, these different stories can be sent in as simultaneous submissions to those editors that accept work that way. Most Writer's Guidelines will spell this out for you, however if they do not, it is best to query about it.

The importance of maintaining careful records is so you will not resubmit the same letter to a publisher who may have rejected it earlier. The manuscript submission logs will assist you in keeping matters straight. Make numerous copies of the blank forms and fill them in as you use them. Remember, if you run out, we can supply you with more.

Here are excerpts from just a few Writer's Guidelines:

"Please do not use multiple names for body parts, most people call it just one word."

"All manuscripts must be type written, or composed on a word processor, double spaced, and written in the first person."

"The length should vary from no shorter than 2 1/2 pages."

"We do not accept simultaneous submissions."

"Include your social security number with each submission."

"TERMS: Payment made is on publication."

"Letters must be at least three full pages long."

"We are looking for well plotted, developed, erotic fiction."

"Manuscripts must be clearly written and easy to read."

"All characters must be eighteen years of age or older."

"All manuscripts must be accompanied by a SASE."

"Word count: 2500-4000 Double-spaced"

"Pay Scale: $ 350-$500 upon publication."

"Bad spelling is one of the most common causes of rejection."

"Introduction: Introduce the characters, and set the scene quickly, without getting too involved in unnecessary details."

These are just a few of the many guidelines editors will expect from you in your submissions.

Chapter 5

Margin Guidelines

As a rule, normally one should leave 1 to 1 1/2 or more inches around any text. Utilize this rule unless your writer's guidelines dictate to you differently. Every publisher/editor will have their way for you to submit your work. Most of the time I print the first page on my letterhead stationery, which contains my name, address, phone, and fax number. I put the title and subject matter first, at the top of the page, and then begin my story. On the next page and those that follow, I print my name and the story title in the upper left corner and then continue the text. Each page is numbered consecutively. At the end of my story, I usually put a few ********* centered beneath it. Next, I print the pseudonym name, or initials I wish to use as the author, then the approximate number of words, and the state the author is writing from. You may also wish to put the rights you are willing to relinquish. Let's pretend this is the last line of a letter/story.

****

Mr. Earl W. Words/Approx/ 750 First North American Rights
New Hampshire
Erotica Author Name An Erotic Story 2
Did you notice what I did above this line? I treated it as though it was the second numbered page of a story. The upper left-hand corner has the author's name and the title printed in it, while the upper right has the consecutive page number. This helps the editor in case the pages get mixed up. They know exactly what story it belongs to, the author, and the proper order of pages.

Remember that each publishing house, and editor that you do business with may want this done a particular way to suite their professional needs. So, you must be willing to be flexible in the marketplace. After a while, you'll submit your work to the same publishers, and it will become easier.

Most editors will want you to at least double-space your lines for editorial reasons. Also try not to begin a page with the last line of a paragraph. What you should do is shorten the previous page, and then bring down two lines or more from the top of the new page you are starting. Also, a good rule of thumb is to have each page of the story contain about the same number of lines.

For lengthier stories, many editors will want you to have a short, two or more paragraph synopsis, explaining the story.

This I do on my letterhead stationery, listing the title, subject matter, number of pages or words, and then the short synopsis.

Chapter 6

Synopsis Example

Erotica Writer

111 Main Street Anytown, USA Zip Code 111-555-1212 Fax 111-555-1213

Mr./Ms. Editor

Adult Publishing Company

111 Broad Street Anothertown, State, Zip Code USA

Month, Day, Year

Dear Mr./Ms. Editor: Please find the enclosed manuscript for your review:

COLLEGE GIRLS. 10 pgs. Words/Approx/400 Lesbian First Time

Two women, one medium build, the other a real knockout, meet during second semester at Ivy league university, while on the cheer leading squad. Soon they manage to become roommates in the same dorm, and spend off-hours, as well as many long evenings exploring all sorts of female/female sexual experiences.

The knockout is rather conservative in her lovemaking, while the medium sized one has all sorts of kinky inhibitions to offer her newfound playmate. Many a wildly erotic escapade is described for the reader.

Please use the pseudonym I have given, Ms. M. Erotica, or one of your own choosing. Please do not utilize my real name.

A SASE enclosed.

Thank you,

Signature of Erotica Writer

Erotica Writer

Chapter 7

Research

Many of you have referred when you ordered the course, concerning specialized areas of interest. This is fine if you like writing about a particular subject matter. Keep in mind the fact that although you may become an expert writer on specialized subject matter/niche, your market may be quite limited. You must not only always be ready to diversify your writing, yet also the markets to which you submit.

For instance, as you do research on publishing houses, always look for other salable opportunities in publications. Study the classified ads and send to those that may be potential clients for your work. Many first-rate publications carry ads for newsletters about specialized subject matter. Those newsletters carry ads for individuals who enjoy that subject matter. So, a publication can lead you to a newsletter, which can lead you further to individual markets. Perhaps eventually you will have enough material written to sell privately through ads. Anything is possible.

Do not rule out the foreign publication market, even though the postage may be slightly higher. The international market covers the entire world. Write to them for Writer's Guidelines also. Then there are also the electronic adult bulletin boards available to computer users. You might sell your stories in disk format or printed out on paper. You might offer customized story disks priced by a fixed amount per story. Consider even one dollar per story with twenty-five on a disk. You can sell copies of the disk for twenty-five dollars, plus shipping, and the original cost of the disk. Plus, you can easily change the contents at no cost.

Online e-publishers, such as the one you obtained this book from, are yet another current example of where you might sell your work.

The more you write, the more you will begin to envision the endless possibilities for sales that exist out there. You not only have to be creative in your writings, yet also in your search to market them. Often,

I would purchase over $ 50.00 worth of adult publications at one time, to get the names, and addresses of the editors. Not only did I acquire the Writer's Guidelines, yet also the way to purchase back issues for writers at a reduced rate. Plus, I got to read what types of stories they were buying. Then there were the classifieds, and printed ads inside that I answered, offering yet more opportunities.

My initial $ 50.00 investment always paid off. Plus, the magazines could then be traded for others, as you network the system to your advantage. The ones you traded for can be traded again, and again. All the while you are obtaining priceless information for your writing business. I cannot stress enough, how important research is, when it comes to writing.

You can imagine all the publications out there that contain some sort of story, not to mention the newspaper tabloid types, with all sorts of stories and ads. Sometimes you do not know where to begin. Many publications are simply informative directories, listing countless subject matters that individuals are interested in. It is all part of research. You must not only write and edit carefully, yet research carefully too.

It may make more sense to start out with the smaller, lessor known publications, as their demands may not be as strict for writers, as some of the more well-known mainstream publications. Always keep in mind that many of these publishing houses move, or go out of business, with many merely changing the corporate name for necessary expansion. So, you must be willing to keep searching for new forms of outlet constantly, thus insuring your greater marketability of your creative work. As a continuing source for new markets, we would like any of you who discover new publishing houses to contact us, so we may add them to the list of publishers, for future editions of this course.

If you are new at this, test the waters with your work, and see how the editors respond. On the other hand, if you have been writing for some time now, and merely wish to find avenues to solicit your work, try the big boys. You'll find out soon enough, whether they like what you write. Just remember this, there is always a market out there somewhere for you. It could be an adult magazine, newsletter, or tabloid, or perhaps individuals who wish to read your work privately. Erotic pen pal groups do exist, not to mention the computer bulletin boards. You'll just have to spend the time and try to see what is out there that satisfies you, as an adult erotica writer. Writing longer length books may be where your talents lie, who knows until you try.

Other areas of writing in the adult market are video reviews, script writing for videos, and telephone dialogues. Many publications will pay you in free adult videos for your time reviewing them, but you'll have to query them first. Toning your work down might allow you to write for more mainstream romantic magazines, and novel publishers. There is also the adult greeting card market, which uses more humorous erotica, but pay good money for one liner. You can always create your own niche market, as I did with this course. There is no reason why you cannot compile all your best stories to offer them for sale through classified advertisements in various publications. There are infinite ways if you just put your creative mind to work for you. By diversifying, it enables you to get away from writing the same sort of material. For instance, I also enjoy writing one liner for adult greeting card companies. Right now, I am also reviewing amateur videos for several national adult publications.

By researching numerous publications, you will begin to see just how many arenas there are to successfully market your own writing in. Opportunity is out there, it is up to you to do your own research, seeking out what offers are the most financially rewarding to you, the writer.

Another area of research is rejection letters. If you receive one without any mention of why it was not accepted, write back, sending a copy of the rejected piece, and ask the editor to let you know precisely why it was rejected. There is always the chance it can be rewritten and sold to them. It happened to me, and the story was finally sold.

Persistence does pay off. If a publisher constantly rejects your work, find out why, and rewrite it, or submit more stories, until they do accept you as an author. You have so much to offer, as the demand for stories is positively out there.

Chapter 8

Creating A Story Line

Idea gathering, and brainstorming are very important when creating the beginning part of your letter, or story. Having an idea file is quite useful, since you can look at the list of possibilities, and choose one that serves your immediate needs. Again, the list can simply be a running sheet of paper, index cards, a small notebook, or a computer file containing story titles, and subject matter, with perhaps a brief synopsis of what the story may be about.

Add more story ideasXXX

Here is an example:

BEST FRIENDS Lesbian

2 roommates begin an affair during second year of college. Both are cheerleaders, a blonde and a brunette. One normal build, the other well endowed. One is kinkier than the other, and always enjoys being in command.

You can see how this can get you started on your way, and then you keep adding, or subtracting ideas to it. It does give you a starting point. Ideas for letters can come from everyday experiences. Try using familiar surroundings, or names and places to set the mood. If you ride the bus every day, you might work a bus ride into a story, or perhaps where you work, including the type of work you do into the story line, with extra fantasies added to it. Often, using areas you are familiar with can make writing easier, as you are already comfortable with the people, and surroundings.

Let me give you an example of how many stories can be derived from one simple statement or idea.

MASTURBATION: Man alone, woman alone, man with woman, woman with another woman, man with another man, 2 women 1 man, 2 men 1 woman, an orgy group performing for each other, a private show, doing it for someone, or having someone do it to them or both, older and younger, relatives, mixed husbands and wives, public displays, dominated and forced, mixed with any form of fetishes, various techniques, and what they use, is it videotaped, are they spied upon unknowingly, are they caught by someone, and have to explain, or now under their control, were they spying, or watching someone to stimulate them, do they do it in some unusual way, is phone sex involved, where is it being done? What is done with the come? All can create countless scenarios for a story on just one subject matter.

So, as you can see, one rough idea can be translated into numerous stories, all sellable. How many did you find from the previous example? I counted close to thirty different stories you could have created from one word. Also, you can just change the original subject matter to create thirty more stories, because the same combinations of people, places, and events can be collaborated into the text.

Remember you are that vivid minded individual that answered the classified ad, so put that money making mind of yours to work for you. Start thinking and creating basic ideas right now to write about later. I told you that in no time you would have more ideas than you could write about.

Another good rule is to always have a small notebook nearby, in case an idea pops into your head when you least expect it. This is true at night, always have one close by your bed. Sometimes before going to sleep is an excellent time to contemplate some story line scenarios in your mind, as you relax. You'll be amazed at how many you can conjure up. A small tape recorder can also come in handy when you want to store a brainstorm, and do not want to write it down.

Just because you can imagine a terrific story, and you decide not to write down some notes concerning it, may be very disappointing. The next time you sit down to write you might just realize you cannot remember that terrific fantasy and must start all over again. It is much easier to look at your own notes, and decide not to use them, then it is not being able to recall that erotic story, which you did not make any notes for.

Once you have chosen your story line, and begin writing, start simple in developing the contents. Just get the basic idea down on paper. Reread it occasionally to make sure it is making sense, and you have not drifted off in another direction. If you have, then that area might make for a completely different story in the future. On the other hand, perhaps you can rework it into your current story. This gives the reader a story within a story. I cannot stress enough about how important it is to keep your writing very uncomplicated in the beginning. You can always rework it. Remember, there is always time to write that perfect, lengthy erotic novel, once you've mastered the basics.

Let us suppose you have written a three-page story about an erotic experience between two people. If it is hot, and you are completely satisfied with the content, then you may submit it as is. Or you can go back through it and begin to lengthen it. Remember longer stories usually pay more money and are not that difficult to write.

For example, you can start by being much more descriptive about the two people, and where all of this takes place. Describe the time of day, weather conditions, the look of the room, and the furniture in it. Get out your thesaurus, and dictionary, and begin to elaborate on the words you have used. Is the eroticism hot enough, or can you be even more sensually descriptive with it. Is this one moment enough for them, or could you expand by adding another character, or form of eroticism for them to perform next. What if there was a twist in the plot? Perhaps the couple could be related, or even husband and wife, merely having a sexual fantasy acted out by each of them, for both. Be advised that relative sex acts are taboo, and illegal in many states, and countries. As I mentioned before, always write legally.

Maybe it is a Friday night, and they have the rest of the weekend together. Can you begin to see how much more involved, and interesting the story can evolve to? This is part of the fun of writing erotica. You are in complete control of the story, and all the characters in it. They are your characters to do with, as only you, the writer, sees fit.

Keep in mind that when you begin, it may be easier for you to just write short letters. This is fine, since only a few short letters bring the same dollar amount as a longer one. By writing shorter letters it will nurture your creativeness and give you a wider variety of plots to explore. Once you have sold shorter letters, it will make writing lengthier stories that much easier now that you have been published.

Just pretend you are describing some fantasy to someone else, and the words should just flow. Another plus, is the fact that you will spend less time writing if you are pressed for time, allowing you to create short works in your free time. Be aware that there are those times when writer's block hits all of us, but look on the bright side, it only emphasizes the fact we are writers.

We will touch upon this shortly. You may want to keep copies of letters you submit so you can refer to them for inspiration, and see how you are developing, as a writer of eroticism. It also depends on the rights you relinquish with your work. If you do not sell all the rights, then you are able to resell your work, so definitely keep your original copies.

I once wrote a letter style story and submitted a follow up version to the editor. In other words, I wrote it as though I was the same person writing in with another erotic experience to share with my readers. You must explain these types of creative avenues to your editor for their response. Some may allow it, while others won't. Once you begin selling your work, you will find indefinite avenues to guide your characters along into one outrageous sexual scenario to another, leaving your readers begging for more.

The editors will be writing you for more submissions, describing what sort of subject matter they are in immediate need of. Then, the sales almost become guaranteed if you deliver the goods they desire.

It certainly is easier sending in manuscripts about subject matter the editor requested.

Always remember, to reread the stories to see if they are exciting to you, because if not, then they are more likely not very exciting to the editors who you send them too. Once again, I cannot impress upon you enough, the importance of professionalism. Please take the time to see that the story text has all the words punctuated and spelled properly. Be sure you do not change character names, or descriptions midway through the stories, or take off on a wild tangent that had nothing remotely to do with the original story line. Also, what person is telling the story might change, and the tenses. I know whenever I begin to type too fast that I transpose letters, add, or delete some, and usually always forget to make the I a capital I. You, the writer, must always be extremely careful when rereading and editing your work. Take the time to review it a few times, before sending it off to the publisher. It will be time well spent. When necessary, you can hire an editor.

Chapter 9

Description & Mood

Do not just write wham bam stories all about sex, spend time to set the mood, and lead the character, or characters through your stories, as you wish. Describe the characters, name them, elaborate on their manner of dress, their smells, how the room looks and feels to them. How is it lit? Is it warm or cool? Keep in mind, however, that too much detail can ruin a good story. For example, if one of your characters is an older and heavier female, be sure to describe her in a pleasing manner to your reader, allowing them to create a picture of her in their own minds. Saying she is rather plump, or somewhat heavy sounds much better than obese or just plain fat, even if you are writing for a publication that specializes in heavier ladies. Also, an older woman, even in her later years sounds better than describing her as 70 years of age, doesn't it? Take a minute and consider how you might write about what a 70-year-old 300-pound woman looks like, to appeal to your readers.

Keep your stories hot, using variations of the sizzling words, contained on the lists later in this course book. I purposely listed them out of alphabetical order so you would search through the lists. This way you might find one you had not considered and use it. Plus, by scanning the lists, the words will become more familiar to you. Use the dictionary, and thesaurus as often as possible.

Read the works of other authors, to study the variety of ways there are to describe a setting, or character. When sitting around with your friends, have each one describe the place you are at, and see the different reaction each one has. You can always go back, and add, or even subtract variables from your stories. After all, it is your work. As the writer, you have creative artistic licensing.

The extra time, and effort you spend on your story before it is sent in, will save you time afterwards. Even if a rewritten story is finally accepted, you still had to take the time to rewrite it, when you could have been working on another one. Remember, if you were to write one story a day, at the end of the year you would have a collection of 365 sellable works. Keep in mind that, as long as seven stories a week are written, no matter when, you have averaged one story per day. It is good to set some type of goal with your writing, so you have a target to strive for.

Chapter 10

Writer's Block

A much publicized, and well-known demon in the writing profession is writer's block. This is when, no matter how hard you attempt it, the words just do not flow. When this happens, just walk away, and try another time. You may find that your thoughts are not flowing on a particular story perhaps because of the subject matter. First, try writing a story about another subject matter. Go back into your story ideas file and chose one that you feel you can write about. This is another good reason for having a story idea file. If you still cannot create a story, then it is time for you to occupy your mind with something else.

Often the blockage is only the subject matter, and characters you are dealing with, and can be overcome by another story line situation. At other times, you will find that you cannot write fast enough to keep up with the creative ideas flowing from your mind. That is how it is at times, feast, or famine. So just roll with the flow and keep at it. Remember, you are creating money with your mind.

When writer's block does hit, fill your time by creating a list of new story ideas. At least this way your time is spent doing something constructive towards your writing. If you are in the middle of a story, and run out of steam, just stop. You can always go back, and resume writing later. That is another one of the beauties of writing, you can do it as often as you like, not when someone tells you to. I always have numerous stories going at the same time, on file in my computer.

This way I always have something to work on, and when writer's block raises its ugly head, I simply begin more. Sometimes it is good just to create a story line, a title, and a few lines to describe what the plot is, and perhaps a few characters. Then leave it and go develop another. You will find that by taking the time to create each mini story line that you will be using your creative writing energies. Plus, this way you will never need a new story to begin. A finished story to a writer is like money in the bank.

Chapter 11

Pseudonyms

Something you budding writers may consider is a pseudonym for those longer manuscripts that are purchased as lengthier stories. Due to the length, it obviously will not be a letter, first person scenario. As it becomes more expressive and intricate, the editor may assume you wish your name printed as the author. This is where you write either at the beginning of story, end of story, or in your cover letter, the fact you wish to use a pseudonym of either there, or you're choosing. If you choose it, make sure you print it for them with the story. This arises when, perhaps you write a lengthy story on a certain subject matter you do not wish your name associated with. Most often your letter style material will use first name, and last initial, and state you included, not a full name, for the author. Samples of these kinds of letters can be found later in this book.

As much as we would like to believe that all we read is true, many times the adult erotica fantasy stories, and letters written are mostly by people like us, freelance authors, who do it for the money. Perhaps some are true, but we never know exactly which ones are, as opposed to those that are professionally written. This opens the doors for horny folks to make money with their vivid minds, by writing sizzling, erotic, sexy stories that sell. So, cash in on it now.

The more experienced you become with your writing, the more opportunities you will discover. For instance, you might begin to write for various publications that cater to specific sexual subject matter. Let's face it, you know you can write about heterosexual situations. If you base most of your stories from this viewpoint then all you need to do is modify the characters, and their actions. Yet you may not want your real name associated with this, or if you are a female writing a story from a male point of view, you will need to have a male name as the author, and vice versa.

Many times, I use the same pseudonym, as the author of my books to create an author that the readers might like to follow. Once you have a recognizable name that readers know, then hopefully they will purchase your books on a regular basis. This is also called a pen name, in writing.

Chapter 12

Payment

As your Writer's Guidelines arrive you will begin to realize the vast difference in payment amounts, and methods. Many publishers have varied rates for varied length manuscripts. Longer length pieces normally bring more money, but just a few smaller length pieces can bring the same amount of payment. It just depends on what you feel more comfortable writing, letters, or short stories. Often, a long letter will bring more money, depending on the publisher. Some may only wish to barter your work for products they sell, or copies of their publications.

Remember, this method can increase your range of research by scanning the other ads in their publications. Many products for barter are not necessarily publications, other adult videos, and products might be available. Some may offer cash value amount, and a trade value amount for your work. Usually, the trade amount will be more. Do not rule out the possibility of trading an amount of your work for a subscription to a specific publication. Always know the type of payment, and the amounts before you submit your finished work to a publishing company, because it can save you valuable time, and postage if their payment rates are not acceptable to you.

Most publishers make payment upon publication of the story, and will send you a free copy of the magazine it appears in. You may have to request a free copy; in case they did not mention it. The copies of your work in print may serve as tear sheets so you might copy them, and send to potential clients, showing them that your work has been published. That free copy also allows you to see what sort of writers they are publishing and allow you to understand just what type of written material they purchase regularly. There is much to be learned from the free publications you receive, so use them wisely. Remember that these free, publications, can be traded for other ones simply by networking.

Keep in mind, that although you receive an acceptance letter, your work will be published in a particular monthly edition. You may have to send a letter of payment inquiry to the accounts payable department if you do not receive payment when you had expected. It is extremely important to keep accurate records concerning this and review them at the beginning of each month to see if you have any outstanding accounts that owe you money. Usually, a letter of inquiry is all it takes. Also, when bartering your work, do not allow the amount owed to get too high. Use the credit, and order from them, even if you trade it to someone else or give it as a gift. Keeping accurate records also helps you to know what editor has bought which story. This way you will not make the mistake of submitting or selling it to another editor.

This brings us to rights. Always find out what rights each publisher is purchasing from you. If you retain your reprint rights, you can resell the piece later. Selling First North American Serial Rights allows you to resell your work. If you sell all rights, you lose them, but many publishers pay more for these. So, investigate this matter carefully, before selling your work. For information concerning rights, contact: The Office of Information and Publications, Library of Congress, Washington, DC 20559, Copyright Office, Public Information Specialist. Also check reference materials in the library, concerning rights. I cannot emphasize enough the importance of researching these rights. So please investigate them further and understand what you are selling.

You may wish to sell your work to other sources once it is published, and you still retain the rights to resell it. Another alternative is to sell your works yourself as a collection, either in printed form, computer disk, or even a high technology CD ROM. Don't forget the Internet as a possible outlet. You may prefer a particular subject matter or two, about which you write exclusively. Advertise your goods in publications that cater to that specific form of sexual titillation, and sell direct, rather than through publishing houses.

Many publications will allow you free ad space for writing stories for them. The choice is yours, once you accumulate enough sellable work, and experience in the marketplace. Today the United States, tomorrow the world. Even foreign publications are anxious to purchase your work.

As for myself, I write whenever I can get the chance, keeping long lists of new story ideas. My goal is one story per day, just so long as I have at least seven new manuscripts ready to mail out every Monday. I submit countless stories to my editors, so they always have an ample amount on hand to choose from throughout the year. Then if they are short of a particular subject matter, they contact me asking to submit this type to them. Also, they will contact me, informing me of new publications that they are about to create. So, I can get the jump on my competition and submit to them before they even reach the stores, and newsstands throughout the country.

There is nothing wrong with writing to an editor every once and awhile, asking if they need any specific story lines. Offer your willingness to supply the needed material to them in your next submission. This keeps your name in front of them for recognition, and allows you information, as to what they are seeking to purchase. Isn't it easier to write your next few stories about subjects they are looking for rather than ones they may have a surplus of?

Also, if you have just received a payment, or acceptance letter recently, it is a nice gesture to thank them for it in your letter. Many publications accept letters to the editors where you can get some additional exposure for your writing, not to mention having the editor know who you are. Just do not become too bothersome, as I mentioned previously in the course, professionalism always works the best.

The most important piece of advice I can relay to you is, keep writing. Do not become discouraged, it is merely an occupational hazard to us writers. There is always a need for fresh writers with new and expanding ideas. That is where you come in, so get busy, and begin writing today, tonight, this very minute if you wish, whenever you have spare time. That is the first, and most important step. Just do it, now. Keep dogging at it, until you receive that first acceptance letter in the mail detailing the amount of your work that has been purchased, and for how much. It is a very good feeling indeed, making you want to sit down immediately to write more sellable stories for that editor, and their publication. Nothing beats the feeling of receiving a check in the mail.

Chapter 13

Sample letters & Submission Logs

Letterhead Sample

Writer's Name

February 27, 2000

Recipient's Address

Dear Editor:

Type your letter here. You might also include a graphic.

Sincerely,
Writer's Signature

Phone: Fax: Email: [Email Address]

Writer's Guideline Query Letter Sample

(Writer's Logo, Name, Address, Telephone & Fax Number go here, depending on design some may be along bottom portion of the page.)

Mr./Ms. Editor
MAGAZINE/Publishing Company
Address
Ciyt/State/Zipcode
Date
Dear Mr./Ms. Editor:
I am a writer of adult erotica and would like a copy of your Writer's Guidelines and payment rates sent to me. Also, information on how I might receive a copy of your publication at a discounted, writer's research rate.
Enclosed you will find a SASE for your convenience.
Your time is greatly appreciated, and I look forward to working with you in the future.
My   signature   states   I   am   at   least   21   years   of   age
_____.

Thank you,
SIGNATURE
Writer's Name

Cover Letter Sample

(Writer's Logo, Name, Address, & Telephone/Fax Number goes here. Some parts may be along bottom of page depending upon the design.)

Mr./Ms./Editor

MAGAZINE/Publishing Company

Address

City, State, Zipcode

Date

Dear Mr./Ms. Editor:

Enclosed you will find my latest manuscript submissions for your publication. They are as follow:

TITLE No. of pgs. Approx/Words/ 0000 Subject Matter

TITLE No of pgs. Approx/Words 0000 Subject Matter

(List all the stories that you send, depending on what editor and publication accept at one time.)

(Also, if they have recently accepted your work or sent you a payment check, make sure you mention it, and say thank you.)

Please inform me if there is any subject matter you are in urgent need of at this time, in order that I may write on that specific subject, for my next submission.

SASE enclosed for reply.

Thank you,

SIGNATURE

Writer Name

Writer's Guidelines Query Sheet Log

Publisher/Magazine Address Date Sent Date Received

1. This can be done on lined paper. Each line has the above information on it. This way you have a record of which publishers you have contacted and their reply or not.

1. Publisher/Magazine. Address. Date Sent. Date Received

Manuscript (Letter/Story) Submission Log
Publisher/Magazine Address Date Sent Reply Date Comments

1. This can be done on lined paper also. Each line will have the above information on it. I suggest you have a separate page for each individual story, so you do not double submit any. Publishers do not like double submissions sent to them, plus you know what story you submitted and do not have multiple submissions. The same story submitted to multiple publishers.
2. Publisher/Magazine Address. Date Sent. Reply Date. Comments
3. Publisher/Magazine. Address. Date Sent. Reply Date. Comments

Letter/Story Sold Log
Title Publication/Editor Date Sold Date Paid Check# Amount $

This can be on lined paper also. It allows you to follow closely what stories have sold and to which publishers. Many publishers do not mind publishing a story that has already been published. It will be in their guidelines. So, there may be a time where you can resubmit some of your stories to other publishers.

1. Title. Publisher/Editor. Date Sold Date Paid Check# Amount$
2. Title Publisher/Editor Date Sold Date Paid Check# Amount$

Chapter 14

Sexciting List Of 1080 Words That Sizzle

Please note, most of these words are descriptive, which will allow for smoother flowing stories. As for the more graphic, sexual words, I leave that up to you, THE EROTICA WRITER. Please forgive me if there are any duplicate words here. Once you see how many there are, you can increase them substantially with the use of a thesaurus, which I highly suggest you have either a printed version, or online version. Both would be best.

charming bubbled nudge twitched chiseled
nutting dampened swipes tempo oily
greasy scattered bloated fluttered mashing
valve coated maddening husky plowed
reeking satiny drawing blunt invitingly
squishing matted beefy navel itchy
straddled crooning trapped jabbed flat
whined tormenting torturous tracing clenched
captured relaxed thrashing digging proportioned
uninhibited dreamlike statue charged profound
magnificent skillfully plugging cuddling unimaginable
meager edge blushed jelly sandwiching
compounded dilated foxiest skewer scraped
shake crack face elastic drawstrings
toys batteries paddle whine mount
stirrups entered excited fuming mad
crazy intent irritated dry social
asleep prone askew riled balanced
awkward frenzied luscious splendid tempestuous
salivating eager wanton villain naughty
chubby fat rounded dimpled sweeping
hunger clean carnivorous pampered powdered
damp sprayed stream liquid continuous

climactic teetered web-like closely cocoon
slick upright feminine masculine clean shaven
dynamic in control dominating slave conquered
connected dug into painful surrender panic stricken
flimsy unrelenting love romantic stranger
tilted tweaked pinched flaring goose bumps
lanky girth pleaser heavy plump
weight fat rolls lard ass ripples fleshy
gelatin quake shake bony skinny
slim around beg frown sorrow
happy thong screamed aloud loud
farted urine pissed anal pried
butt backside bruised curled unfurled
velvety raspy sissy stinking sweating
rough texture coarse satiny reeling
in out on top under against farther
across navel spread wider agape
control spilled shrank shriveled drew
surrounded filled entered emptied blonde
brunette redhead curly straight short
long bobbed foreigner accent soft spoken
whisper yell shrieked loud voice bellowed
growled obey demanded confused barked orders
dizzy sleeping awake suspended lightheaded
jumping devilish evil gentle commanding
shivering calloused smooth rough grainy
tough pale shallow pink dark
reddened bouncing gyrating tense encircled
entwined erased lady like frail puffy
off balance heavy breathing bizarre kinky
nimble delicate dare devil lewd mischievous
tart talk dirty vile shame canyon

variety peaks giddy tickled nostrils flared
felt quickly grabbed thrust full figured
doll like rant & rave convulsing porcelain skin
torn touched shadows pivoted sprang
awoke clambered appeared bathed showered
released sprinkled anointed diaper soiled
sickly ran groped pointed upright
firm natural filled high cheek boned
powdered stinks stunk awful stink smell
odor oral glistening beautiful shimmering
gorgeous like it not another spectacular one of a kind
spilled pleasant tired exhausted expressed
lewdly perverse held holder container
plunged rammed jammed rode ride
ran writhed moaned enticing amazon
lengthy huge torso lanky bold
bald rip climbed hastened hastily
quietly shuddered shear thin see through
crotch less shaved crew cut streaked bleached
platinum wavy glasses thick tipped more
scar stitches contrasting negative nothing
not a thing balled up thrown heaved swung
swing flaunt flirt hussy demon like
rapture titillating promise decadent forceful
bullying aggressive submissive restraints locked
handcuffs shivering enough laughing shaking
weeping wedged whimpering teary eyed rapid pulse
stared slobbering form peculiar eyed
quickly gleefully raced devoured hindered
undress hasten eagerly awarded pranced
danced bumped ground humped hid
ached arched hiding gladly eager

skillfully snuggled underside beneath pre
stain helpless caress feel throbbing
begging first time virgin climax pumping
weeping hole seeping cried out masturbate
played with increased lover frigged swelled
enlarged growing swelled heaving raspy
shallow thralls ecstasy forgiveness temptations
tantalizing effort towering expanding effortless
sweltering relish satisfaction raving grunting
continuous ravishing hounded kindness raw
sore exposed pulled stroked pivoting
yanked shaft drew gyrations staggering
fallen bent crooked limp straight
narrow wandering juicy saucy lathered
shove drink guzzle brazen spew
spit naked nude bare flesh bit
bite bitten gnawed swallow drank
raised suck blew lower drop
remove clasp zip unbutton nook
paddled massive broad short extremely tall
little tiny dark swaying loose
tight hump wicked repulsive heated
sap hideous breath smack rose and fell
twitched fingered sank turned crawled
lay bent over reclined lie amazed
smile horror spank cringing pouted
pouring fear frustration nonstop never ending
increasing endless relentless scampered agonizing
taught coaxing anxious mounds pouting
vacuuming open gaping cavernous agitated
stimulation spying unable voyeur peeping
spicy not kinky passive shy

gentle dirty dominant gross slutty
thick sky tidal wave torrential runny
broad big monumental wrinkled matronly
wiggled giggled melons jiggled Rubenesque
lengthy long soft tender hard
tangy pulsating rigid dangling erect
firm hairy squeezed manhandled smooth shaven
pimpled brown bottom flappy lips feet
ankles toes teased touched tickled
bound tied tormented roped gagged
suspended released explode escaped wax dripping
taunted tortured moist saliva lick
moisture beads sweat licked ate
hunger slithered nippled tongued rubbed
sweltering blister willfully languished soulful
constant shivering rolled tingling aroma
spent enveloped evolved large lady spindle
spiral statuesque crept sneaky satisfaction
lavish waves of pores surrendered lava like flow
rosebud flower like exquisite genteel studs
learner latex spikes metal chrome
conspiracy feather fur confident contradicting
creature buzz come sluts matted braided
limber pliable oils potions lotions scantily clad
ushered up in the air massaged addicted indulgent
on all fours caressed carelessly dense contempt
ribbed sexy swept rained slippery
wet horny slender wiry ripe
vixen sensual sinister subtle succulent
skinny flopping oozing savoring encore
experience tasting heated cavity tramp
oiled flipped catlike lubricating spirited

noisy showered bathed did not behave
wrapped loosely tied fooled manipulated
regretted hiding unaware cramped unknowingly
fatigued grew endowed gifted camouflaged
captivating charming simple survived painlessly
numb quivering shining riveted astonishing
rocked spanning reeled roped contorted
balanced ability contortions brought dungeon
eerie effort pierce safe sex happy
fluids orgasmic orgasm whip lashed
clips clamps clothes pins weights twisted
tweaked sallow reddened crimson welts
videos nudes nude photos amateur adult
adults only baby taboo brats man of house
milk milking hand feet face
head skin clothed lingerie bra
panties t backs thongs lace granny panties
LGBTQ lesbian queer gay transgendered
transexual transvestite shemale bisexual sapphic
lipstick package junk booty butch
macho role play adults only amateur man of the house
videos nudes photos brat photography
cameras porn websites webcams erotic
webcams content threesomes couples married
single sellers writers readers erotica
dumped squatted laid finally coaxed
instigated attached withheld privacy communal
fiery fierce maniac sharp numbing
candy sweet sour vulgar ugly
pretty minuscule pathetic wimp unstoppable
conniving peers subjected valued meaningless
sex toys sex dolls rubber strap on beads

vibrate spit age gap cougar showers
golden glistening ass anal starfish
areola nipples pinched branded without touching
succession agonizing favorite peeking watching
looking leaving teased pleased believed
coincidence liable liar mistake BDSM
bondage submit dominant punish raw
slid fuzzy rash pimples on myself
diagonal round odd shaped rapid reaction
vomit padded sharp dull chains
become lady like feminine glassy wide eyed
sashay sauntered perfumed stale dank
dusky musky rank funk uncircumcised
member comical caned slapping flaps
related relative carnal scapegoat guilty
beefy skinny slim slender overweight
chubby bosom bubble chance knelt down
vulnerable breasts breeding pregnant frail
failed crying embarrassed excuse false
crack fungus infection erection detection
perfection dreaming hypnotic magical trash
first premiere envy dangerous beautiful
stacked staggering inside outside exhibitionist
animalistic duly begging outcast homeless
vagrants examples checked out bedroom hotel
motel professional hooker wanton make out
make up all alone together single solo
feel dimples teeth bite saw
sore simple ginger natural foolish
smart tear unfastens remove given
cool demanding senile grimy volumes
cold stagnant pure degenerate climaxed

semen came exploded dripping ended

These should get you started on your way to writing descriptive erotica of all kinds. Forgive me if there are a few duplicates in here. I did reread it numerous times, and even add a few more afterwards.

As I mentioned before always take advantage of a thesaurus whenever you can. It will make your work much more interesting and never repetitive and have your erotica readers asking you for more. Happy erotica writing writers.

Remember I invite all of you to contact me with any question you may have about erotica writing. Visit my website, Dm me on social media, or just email me bbpierceauthor@yahoo.com

Chapter 15

Greeting Cards & Adult Oriented Humor

Being a writer affords one the flexibility to make money in numerous arenas. Writing for the adult market is one arena, the romance market is another, and still yet there is the greeting card market. Here, one can even venture further by tapping into comedy, poetry, and simple everyday copy. Happily, there is money to be made in all these varied areas. In one day, you can sit down, and create text for all these markets. The adult greeting card market is simply one more avenue to travel.

That is what is so fantastic about being a writer, you can write whatever you want, when whenever you want to, writer's block aside. The general principals you learned earlier in the erotica writing course still apply, always be professional. You will have to send for Writer's Guidelines, and follow up with query letters, and keep accurate logs about your work. Only now with greeting card writing, you can submit one liners for the comedy market. The difference is they may request you have only one card copy on a 3" x 5" index card, or one greeting card line to a sheet of paper. Once again, each publisher has a set of guidelines to adhere too. You can also write comedy scripts for a change of pace.

You may want to visit the reference section of the library, or local bookstore to see what is on hand concerning comedy writing, as well as rhyming verses. The references from "Writing EROTICA For Fun & Profit" still apply, so utilize them. For research, you just might have to spend some time in the greeting card stores, and reading what is being purchased.

Comedy is also used on bumper stickers, tee shirts, and coffee mugs, just to name a few other places. Look around out there and see just how many places where writers can sell their work. Nowadays, with the shop at home attitudes many folks have, you will see more and more catalogues arriving in the mail. Many of these can become resources in which to sell you writing. The ones offering humorous products are the ones to target with your comedy writing ideas. Another way is to get the manufacturer's name and address from funny products, then contact them directly with a query letter offering your own writing services.

You will have to do some creative resource work, yet it will pay off, once you begin submitting your comedy writing to that specialized marketplace. Again, do not forget to ask for copies of your published work to use as advertising for the type of writing only you can create. It's a nice touch to send along a copy of some of your published work, when seeking additional writing opportunities with editors. This just adds to the fact you are an accomplished writer in that field.

Greeting Card Publisher List:

Amberly Greeting Card Company

11510 Goldcoast Drive Cincinnati, Ohio 45249

Landmark General

51 Digital Novato, CA 94947

Papermoon Graphics

PO Box 34672 Los Angeles, CA 90034

Sunrise Publications, Inc.

1145 Sunrise Greetings Court Bloomington, IN 47401

West Graphics

385 Oyster Point Blvd. Unit 7 South San Francisco, CA 94080

American Greetings Corp.

10500 American Road Cleveland, Ohio 44144

Freedom Greetings

PO Box 715 Bristol, PA 15007

Maine Line Company

PO Box 947 Rockland, ME 04841

Nobele Works

113 Clinton Street Hoboken, New Jersey 07030

Paramount Cards, Inc.

PO Box 6546 Providence, RI 02940-6546

Comstock Cards, Inc.

PO Box 3477 Reno. NV 89505 Also (600 S. Rock Blvd #15)

Intercontinental Greetings, Inc.

176 Madison Avenue New York, New York 10016

Merlyn Graphics, Corp.

Box 9087 Canoga Park, CA 91309

Oatmeal Studios

PO Box 138 Rochester, VT 05767

Sangamon Company

Route 48 West PO Box 410 Taylorville, IL 62568

Peacock Papers, Inc.

273 Summer Street Boston, MA 02210

Rockshots

632 Broadway at Bleeker Street New York, New York 10012-2416

Kalan

97 S. Union Avenue Lansdowne, PA 19050

TLC Greetings

615 Mc Call Road Manhattan, KS 66502

Russ Berrie and Company, Inc.

111 Bauer Drive Oakland, New Jersey 07436

Blue Mountain Arts, Inc.

PO Box 4549 Boulder, CO 80306

No! No! Greetings

PO Box 221 Norco, CA 91760

Greetings Magazine

309 Fifth Avenue New York, New York 10016

The following are geared for comedy:
Post Industrial Press
Attn: Submissions Department
2506 South Fawcett Tacoma, WA 98402
The Imagination Workshop
c/o KANU
Broadcasting Hall
The University of Kansas Lawrence, KS 66045
Modern Greeting & Gag Writing
PO Box 1142 Novato, CA 94947
Comics Career
601 Clinkscales Columbia, MO 65203
Imagineering Inc.
Box 11859 Phoenix, AZ 85061
Comedy USA Newswire
915 Broadway New York, New York 10010
Witty World
Box 1458 North Wales, PA 19454

Chapter 16

Over 250 Story lines

With 250 storyline ideas all of you reading this should come away with at least one great erotica story idea to start writing about. Remember to only write erotica that is Legal, legal, legal always, and never deter from it.

Please refer to the lists more than once. They may help your imagination.

1. Using various types of fruits & vegetables for sexual satisfaction

2. Spanking by, or of another individual, or group

3. Butt plugs, & anal stimulations, & ass worship

4. Utilizing worn, soiled undergarments for additional sexual gratification

5. Older driver picks up hitch hiking military personnel, and drive to motel to have sex, or any other sort of character, or characters

6. Please note that any topic, or idea can be changed to spawn numerous stories. Just imagine love from behind. An anal devotee loves anything, if it is lengthy & thick, plus oral anal too. One sexual position spawn so many stories.

7. Chubby female extremely horny with rolls of fat, chubby chasers

8. Female masturbates in all kinds of ways for video camcorder to sell, and trade

9. Wife makes husband beat off for her friends, both female, and male

10. Male asks women to humiliate, and punish him in all sorts of unspeakable sexual acts, making sure to offer lots or verbal dirty talk humiliation about his size

11. On way back from bathroom niece/step niece catches Uncle/step Uncle beating off, and then demands he eat her etc.

12. Overzealous male/female cock lickers, and their many exciting techniques

13. Wife spanks hubby for female friends' amusement, & invites gay male to do same, as Hubby beats off for them, and then does the male sexually, & disgustingly

14. Two naked people locked in cage, who must struggle to get key for release

15. Males/trannies who can suck themselves off

16. Wife likes to spank hubby, & then squat over his face for oral anal stimulation

17. Female who masturbates for senior citizen who has not gotten hard for long time, he smells her feet, and comes on them, as she sits naked before him rubbing his semi hardness between her bare feet (foot jobs)

18. Dildo sex toy mania of woman or man, with compulsive obsession for it

19. Undress in front of window, knowing neighbor, or someone else out there is watching for erotica exhibitionism

20. Stepsister, & her friends sexually terrorize younger stepbrother, & humiliate

21. Man wears woman's panties to work, and beats off in men's room

22. Sexxy pen pals, and what they write, and suggest to each other in their hot letters. This can also be emails and texts.

1. Female being driven around naked, as she masturbates in back seat for truckers to see.

24. Power toothbrushes on clits, and cocks

25. Tied & tickled for mild bondage games

26. Cat like tongue bathes over the entire naked body, which can be dirty & sweaty

27. Husband finds wife's vibrator, & makes her demonstrate what she does with it

28. Female who loves to play with herself, as often, and as many ways as possible

29. Adults who enjoy diapering and being treated like a baby, Infantilism.

30. Water sports, both giving and receiving, plus self-giving, and exhibitionist

31. Voyeur in small private motel/bed breakfast with peepholes behind the mirrors

32. Sexual stimulation using one's own panties for pleasure

33. Public exposure, whether totally nude, or just flashing at the right moment for excitement, walking totally naked in hotel hallway, down lone dark alleys

34. Using handcuffs during sexual acts, and other forms of restraint

35. Leave panties in men's room, & watch who comes out with them, or leave in buses, cabs, laundry facilities, & strange cars/cabs for others to find

36. Sex partners of various ethnic/racial origins

37. The babysitter, male or female

38. Two older females with a young innocent male for his first time, as sex toy

39. Female domination of male, or other females

40. Stepmom is a tease

41. Picking up the homeless cleaning them up, & wild sexual situations, who is going to know, plus make amateur adult videos, or take nude pix, & pay them

42. Come bathes in face, hair, & all-over naked body parts

43. Eating sausage/hot dogs, and other food from a woman's vagina

44. Escort service sends over a beautiful well-built transexual by mistake

45. Sex with a latex rubber surgical glove

46. Lesbian instructor at an all-girl's school

47. Sex using lotion at an outside cabana at secluded resort, while you are watched

48. Sexy nymph into nonstop sexy bondage

49. One woman & many men to service

50. Erotic neighborhood situations

BONUS: Remember to change the characters & scenarios as often as possible to create additional story lines

51. A massage therapist who makes house calls

52. A nurse who services patients in hospitals, at home, or on special dates

Next series:

1. Wife sits back in recliner lifting, and spreading legs, as husband services both holes

2. Two military men/women on leave in same motel room, become kinky & sexually involved. Either m/f, f/f, mm, and maybe maid joins in?

3. Eighteen-year-old high school friends experiment with each other sexually, same sex, first time having any sort of sex with another individual

4. Girlfriend finally agrees to anal sex, only after donning strap on, and using it on you first, after she has used other items to loosen you up.

5. Getting sexual kicks by being driven downtown late at night, undressing, and walking out to middle of street, or down the block, and then back to car completely naked

6. Older female seduces eighteen-year-old male delivery person, by answering door in only a towel, and carelessly allowing it to fall from her naked, big titted body.

7. Woman who finds numerous ways to pleasure herself with her vacuum cleaner.

8. Bored housewife side lines as hooker on street corner, and begins to like it too much, and soon only enjoys sex if it is

with a total stranger, and on the dangerous side.

9. Young female catches Mother & Aunt having lesbian sex, and gets caught watching them, then is forced to pay the price by answering up to them naked.

10. A man's favorite sex sites on the NET, and how he pleasures himself while viewing them.

11. Decadent man pays homeless to perform for and/or have sex with him on the streets.

12. Toilet training school for bad girls & older men

13. Female employees have revenge on sex harassing boss in many lewd, and vile ways.

14. Older stepsisters humiliate eighteen-year-old stepbrother, after catching him masturbating with their dirty & sexually soiled panties, make him wear them.

15. Skinny man who enjoys being abused by obese woman, especially spanking, and being almost smothered between their fat thighs, as he is made to orally, please them, at both holes.

16. Nurse gets off working in hospital with dirty bedpans, and cleaning patients.

17. Farm worker enjoys it as farmer's daughter pees on him, as he lays in dirty hay in the big barn and allows her to do other unspeakable things with him.

18. Female gets off wearing adult diapers under clothes at work and messing in them.

19. Female tourist on cruise ship takes on most of the foreign male crew members in all sorts of orgy like, and bizarre sexual adventures, both men, & women

20. Man finds female squatter in abandoned house, and takes her home, as his willing sex slave trading her room, and board for sexual favors of all sorts

21. Exploits of a retired man who delivers pizza, and what some

of his last stops have been.

22. Widower runs a boarding house, and only rents rooms to well-endowed females, so he can watch, and spy on them when they least suspect it, they work in nearby strip clubs.

23. Eighteen-year-old girl experiments sexually on herself alone at home in her bedroom

24. Step Uncle/Stepfather catch her, and she is given special lessons after being punished first, with an old-fashioned bare ass spanking.

25. Sexy babysitter takes off her panties, gives to the husband, after he drives her home, and just what he does with them afterwards, and later during her next sitting job. Can also be done with the wife.

26. Young man enjoys being dominated sexually by his mother/ Stepmother, and/or older stepsister.

27. Photographer advertises for nude female models, and some hot sex develops from it.

28. Newlyweds make their first amateur adult video tape during their honeymoon.

29. Grandfather catches his grandson having sex with another male, and becomes excited, and soon joins him.

30. Female in apartment next door gets locks out and must spend the night with neighbor (can be female or male) sleep in same cramped bed, and hot sex results.

31. Man gets off taking female soiled panties from the laundry room in apartment buildings, and at homes of others from their dirty laundry hampers.

32. How a woman soils her panties, so she can sell them through classified ads

33. During red eye flight, a female plays with herself, as man next to her watches, before she later takes care of him as well.

34. Late at night, an older female comes into adult video/

bookstore putting on her own performance for the clerk, and a few happy customers, she enjoys giving oral sex, plus glory hole fun in adult video bookstores.

35. Exploits of a bartender at a female strip club (could be male or female bartender). Same goes for male strip club.

36. Straight female goes to lesbian bar for her first-time lesbian experience.

37. Two lesbians torment & humiliate a macho neighbor, until they feminize him totally, showing him what it is like to sissygasm.

38. Straight male's first experience in an S&M club and goes home with a couple who keep him over the weekend, and do just about everything with him, until he is a changed man.

39. A man's reply to a personal ad in sex magazine gets him much more than he ever bargained for (use your vivid imagination here)

40. Younger wife enjoys her first spanking from her older husband, after she misbehaves, and finds out just how much she enjoys being punished for being a bad girl.

41. Couple enjoy being visible having sex so others in building across from them can watch.

42. A video voyeur captures some bizarre footage searching the windows in his area, which is a large center city apartment co-op building.

43. Lucky limo driver with a horny bachelorette party to drive around all night gets luckier, as they get hornier, and more daring.

44. Female who flashes fast-food drive-in windows, & toll booths

45. Male/female who masturbate on video to sell, and trade them with others, and some they have received in trades.

46. Two females having sex in motel room get caught be pretty young maid, who they seduce to join them for some more

than kinky sexual activities, as they tie her up. Can be the same for 2 men, or man and woman in the room.

47. Female exhibitionist running around mall late at night naked, gets caught by big black security guard, who offers her both his huge cock, and long night stick for his silence.

48. Housekeeper comes in to clean and catches eighteen-year-old male of the house masturbating and teaches him some lessons about female anatomy.

49. Recently divorced man went on blind date with younger female, who demands he tie her up, and whip, and spank her, he is amazed at how hot he gets, and finds a new sexual outlook on life, bondage, and light S&M

50. Male theater professor in small mid-western college has unique dilemma of having to give female lead to either of two young, and more than willing females, one eighteen and pretty, and well built, the other twenty good looking with enormous tits, and well-rounded ass.

51. Bonus Story ideas: Remember to change the characters & scenarios, as often as possible to create additional story lines.

52. Grandfather aged male who calls a telephone sex line and gets help getting off from a pretty young thing, you can write it from either point of view.

53. Man gets seduced by his sister-in-law, who is older, and was married to his brother, and she enjoys more bizarre forms of sex, as his brother had once told him, he soon finds out just how bizarre.

54. Youthful Grandmother takes on her grandson, and his group of rowdies, horny friends on long Friday night.

Next Series:

1. Anal sex, but only using the tongue to insert nothing else, totally oral pleasuring.

2. Sexy bath and/or shower scenario of solo masturbation
3. Young female in college earns extra money posing, and videotaping herself doing naughty, and very nasty things.
4. Three single women go on vacation, and soon find out that they do not have to be lonely, and starved for sex, as they begin sleeping together nude in the same bed.
5. Average looking male does not meet women easily, and answers ad to be sex slave of a very, very domineering female, he gets sex, and never has to worry about social dating.
6. Stories a window washer talks about just a few of the odd, and rather bizarre sexual images he has witnessed, while washing windows in a big city apartment/condo complex
7. Female/male who licks other people's dirty feet clean, and then uses them to pleasure themselves with
8. Female masseuse at a women's spa, who likes women, and offers just a bit more with her sessions to the right women.
9. Skinny tall girl who is only attracted to fatter men who are just slightly older too at times, can make for an unusual sight once they are naked in bed, and how she likes to be taken by them, and often how she enjoys riding them for a change of fast pace.
10. Young couple, eighteen /nineteen, and their first sexual scenario at an outdoor movie drive in theater
11. A Father's daughter with her new, and younger Stepmother who seduces her, while she is at home after a bitter divorce.
12. You (a voyeur) go on vacation and have the good fortune to be staying right next to a nudist resort, and have access to see their beach, and living facilities.
13. A not so usual college sorority initiation as it is a lesbian sorority of the nineties.
14. Customer plays some hot footsies with a kinky foot fetish shoe salesman in a woman's shoe store (Oh my aching feet)

Could also be a woman shoe salesman.
15.   Man, always sneaking peeks at woman's pantyhose, and
      panties up under

dresses, and when legs crossed, or opening until is caught by
one long legged, as she begins to give him just what he wants
(Pantyhose, panty fetish)

1.   Woman/man enjoys their job of cleaning public toilets, and
     what they find in them, and what scenarios they get caught
     up in just by doing their job.
2.   Female hitch hiker accepts ride with older man, then must go
     pee in middle of nowhere, and he watches as she brazenly gets
     out passenger side turns, pulls down pants, and faces him
     peeing, and then what happens later and next time she must
     pee (Wonder what she uses for toilet paper?)
3.   Young male taken care of while bed ridden, his mother/
     Aunt/Grandmother treats him, as she used to, and gets nude
     before stroking him off.
4.   Hitch hiking younger male is surprised when older female
     picks him up, and has mistaken him for male hooker, and
     offers him money for his sexual services. Of course, he
     accepts, and what takes place is far beyond anything he has
     ever experienced sexually.
5.   New girlfriend is not only very intensively orgasmic yet
     extremely loud and dirty mouthed, explain her lewd, and
     loud descriptive behavior to the readers.
6.   Male strokes off in front of window knowing divorcee next
     door might see, as well and unknowingly so does the husband
     of another neighbor in a nearby house, and how either can
     approach him and make him an offer for their silence which
     is why he did it in the first place yet they do not know this,
     and of course he only wanted women to approach him, and

now he has a man to deal with

7. Catch husband cheating, and for his punishment you assemble his close friends, and male co-workers, and have him sit, and watch, as you taunt him by allowing them all to have anal sex with you, his loving wife, then maybe you have anal sex with him receiving.

8. Two brothers, one older teaches younger about sex, and females as he is bi.

9. Sexy pen pal correspondence with numerous pen pals worldwide describing some hot sexual scenarios, and maybe even planning to meet, or the photos they send you, and videos they also send you later of them naked and doing odd things to themselves.

10. Mistress has you come, and keeps it in glass, until full, and then it is ready to drink (maybe she demands you drink it all, shares it with you, or she drinks it herself)

11. Horny wife, and a large, long, black metal flashlight late at night

12. Walking completely naked down the hallway, and back to your door, and unlocking it to go inside, can be done in apartment complex, or large hotel in big city, perhaps you even go down one flight in stairwell, and back up to your room, thought of getting caught so exciting you stroke off wildly (Or maybe you do get caught and have to suffer the consequences?) Male wearing panties?

13. Using yourself, and large sex toy to double penetrate your wife and/or girlfriend.

14. Midget/dwarf/little person sex, either male or female having sex with one, or someone else having kinky sex with them

15. Mild torturous activities, clothes pins on nipples, tickle with feathers, weights clamps to genital areas etc., or bind someone naked at night in front window, and turn on lights, and leave

room with them fully exposed, and visible through window to others in large complex.

16. Female total body shaving, by themselves, or someone doing it for them.

17. Tattoo, body piercing parlor owner with some bizarre tales to talk about his female, and/or male clients, and some fringe benefits he, or she received.

18. Wife give husband oral sex, as he sits on the toilet, or vice versa.

19. Husband enjoys dressing up in his wife's clothing, and gets caught, but by who? His wife, sister, mother-in-law, mother, sister-in-law neighbor female, or maybe another male with similar interests, who knows?

20. Horny over sexed wife seeks out overly well-endowed males of any ethnic background, or race for nonstop hot sex (Maybe her husband watches?)

21. Ex-wife humiliates the new wife in front of her friends, have catfight, and easily dominates her (Head and body shaving possible?)

22. Eighteen-year-old son/daughter peep into parents' bedroom to see that they are far from a normal family, especially when it comes to raunchy, kinky, parental sex.

23. Man's first experience sexually, as a crossdresser from dressing up, and getting ready to going out to be picked up by another man and having m/m sex for first time.

24. Sexual penetration using one finger, then more, and more until your entire hand goes in, but goes in where and in whom? This is up to YOU.

25. Mother seduced by her young lesbian daughter, after daughter confesses to being a lesbian, she shows her mom a hot, and satisfying time.

26. Male salesman seduced on overnight business train ride, but

by whom, a man, or a woman.

27. Man, answers ad placed by a dominating Mistress, and goes to her house, and is completely dominated by her, as she introduces him into the bizarre world of bondage, and S&M, as he becomes her personal sex slave.

28. Wife announces to hubby she wants him to give her an enema, and what happens next (Or vice versa)

29. Campsite ranger comes to the rescue of two female campers, and how they reward him.

30. Sexy young punk rocker female finds a special way to pay her landlord every month, which keeps both quite happy.

31. Retired male gets a job as dishwasher at a strip club and finds he has found his mecca.

32. Man gets excited, as he witnesses another man beating off in public rest room, and what he does about it afterwards.

33. Stern domineering Mother decides her nineteen-year-old son is still not too old to get an old fashioned bare bottomed spanking even in front of.... Her friends, his friends, his girlfriend, or perhaps someone else who might make it even more punishable.

34. A man attracted to dirty, scuzzy, ill kept females, whose smell and dirtiness excites him almost beyond control, after all the dirty girls are all more than happy to have sex with anyone, or anything for that matter, so he has little competition, and much to gain.

35. BONUS: Remember to change your characters around, and forms of sexual activities to broaden your areas for writing even more

36. Having sex with date and finding out she has her period.

37. How one lap dancer found a way to make even bigger tips doing what she liked to do with men. Please note that any topic or idea can be changed or combined to spawn

numerous stories.

1. Businessman meets professional call girl in hotel grill and makes her an offer only to get much more than he had bargained for.
2. First time having sex with another race, and how good it is.
3. Meet someone on INTERNET, and have sexy, and hot email sessions, soon sending photo images before hooking up c-u-c me cameras for mutual masturbation session.
4. Young female's car breaks down on secluded country road, and she seeks shelter in farmhouse with older couple who seem kind and innocent, yet are far from it, as she all too late begins to realize her fate.
5. Run into your ex-husband/wife, who has remarried, yet you still have time for a quickie.
6. Bedridden, and must wear adult diapers, but soon find wetting them is sexually stimulating, and your mate soon realizes how much fun it is to treat you like an adult baby.
7. Your old maid sister comes to stay with you on her week vacation, you are divorced, and lonely seeking sexual gratification, and find it with her.
8. Two cousins always liked each other as children, now all grown up, and both divorced find each other, and have much overdue hot sex.
9. Kinky female who enjoys riding taxis in big city late at night scantily clad, and always pretends not to have enough to pay the fare, thus paying for it with sexual favors.
10. Hot coed one long winter night pulls an all-anal gang bang with a fraternity, or team.
11. One man's sexual attraction to extremely hairy women who have hair on face, arms, legs and especially an over abundant patch between their legs for him to worship.
12. Have sex with soft and sexy foods, by cutting holes into them,

and having sex through them.

13. Male first time goes to peep show booth with glory holes in it and inserts himself through one for oral sex by a complete stranger, and a male at that, as far as he can tell, because the place only had males in it, he saw no females.

14. Female who orgasms rather wet and wild, squirting her inner juices wildly about, as she convulses to one violent orgasm after another, she is insatiable, and always drenching wet.

15. A peeper voyeur who finds places, and ways to look up unsuspecting female's skirts in public places, and public transportation.

16. Man likes wearing girlfriends' undies, and dresses as female one night, and drives around the city, and needs gas so he/she stops at all night service station for a fill up, in more than one way.

17. Older female who enjoys using her bare feet, and big soft tits to masturbate younger men with

18. Custodian in a large metropolitan complex who fixes more than just the squeaky hinges, stuck windows, and poor plumbing for the female residents.

19. Man, dates nurse, and finds she is quite proficient sexually, as well as kinky, and soon she is giving him high colonics regularly, and teaching him how to administer them to her also. Plus, prostate massages.

20. A female foot worshipper who only adores other women's bare stinky feet for them. It can also be male male or male or female worshipping other sexes feet.

21. Kinky husband who enjoys it when after finishing having anal sex with his tall wife, she next straps on her big dildo, and inserts it in him. (Pegging)

22. How things can heat up in a retirement village with the residents, and at certain times of the year when younger

relatives visit, offering some sexxy shows, as well as a few college students who will stop at nothing to earn a few extra dollars doing special favors when, and where they can. Can also be staff.

23. One man's lust for extremely tiny, and skinny females who almost appear mannish in their looks, and manners.

24. Thin men being completely dominated sexually by amazon like, and big fat females who constantly humiliate them.

25. Man describes what he does with soiled panties he buys through the mail, and what the girls look like who sell him their panties, and how they make them dirty for him.

26. Younger male being taught to service a woman giving her oral sex, and how she instructs him what to do, and where to do it to her, as she orgasms all over his face.

27. Male and his uncle has mutual masturbation sessions taking turns getting each other off.

28. Male boss finds a male employee masturbating in men's room, and demands he meet with his gay friends, or suffer exposure to his co-workers.

29. A female librarian at a small college turns out not to be so prim and proper, as one athletic male student finds out firsthand.

30. For his anniversary a man is given his wife who has covered her ass, and pussy with whip cream, and cherries, which he gets to lick completely clean, and then do with her, as only he wishes, she soon learns that she wished she had known of some of these wishes years earlier in their marriage and enjoys their bizarre sexual evening all too well.

31. Younger female secretary is seduced by her older, and powerful female boss only to turn the tides, and soon have her boss begging her for mercy, as she begins to have her own sexual way of fun with her, and soon shares her with others.

32. A female gets off alone, while watching a lesbian video for the first time, and gives us all a vivid description of both her antics, and the video performers.

33. A bitter ex-girlfriend along with one of her female friends place her ex-boyfriend in some highly uncompromising positions, as they dominate him, and turn him up in the air, as he comes so he can have a taste, as she likes to refer to it.

34. Straight male hooker gets picked up by a transexual, only to find out that the customer is always right and finds some new ways of entertaining his clients.

35. Older couple attend a swingers alternative lifestyle type convention for the first time, and experience slightly more than they bargained for, yet soon began to adapt easily.

36. Young female can only become sexually excited if spanked or caned or paddled.

37. Female soils her panties puts them in sealed plastic bags and mails them to her old boyfriends anonymously, so they do not know who sends them, also a few fellow male workers, and female friends to see who mentions it.

38. Older Mother-in-law hot for her middle-aged son in law and seduces him without her daughter's knowledge.

39. Male who gets off by having women allow him to smell their worn shoes, and let him fondle their stocking clad feet, and sniff their worn pantyhose.

40. A kinky female who collects come from men by masturbating them into a pitcher, and drinking the mixture at parties she throws for all her lesbian friends.

41. Homely, yet well-built female adventures when she spent a very long, yet hot winter up in Alaska where the ratio of men to women was in her sexy favors.

42. A real knock out model type sexy female who only gets hot for overweight men, and what she does to meet, and get them

to come back to her place to ravage her.

43. Husband's wife is away on business trip when next door neighbor comes over naked under her coat, and seduces him, while her big burly husband is right next-door watching sports on television.

44. Trucker picks up uninhibited female hitch hiker in rain, and watches as she completely changes in front of him, & then offers to perform oral sex on him, of course he agrees, and that is just the first few miles, as he takes her all the way to where she is going & shares her with some buddies at stops along the way.

45. Male and female sneak into public restroom at airport, and have sex, while others are using it, and unaware of what they are doing in the stall.

46. Male surprises new girlfriend with a huge dildo he plans to use on her, and she surprises him by taking all of it, and begging him for more.

47. Young males nineteen, and older create an athletic ritual, whereby they stand around in a circle with a nude female in the center, and beat off to see which one gets to spend time with the willing female, who often is young, pretty, older, and or ugly, and they vary their coming, such as one time it might be first off, the next is the last off, and then they might pick an odd number, and that person wins the prize

48. Man realizes just how much his new girlfriend is into latex with her provocative way of dressing in it, and seducing him, while wearing it even covering her head, and face with it, while having sex.

49. Husband and wife enjoy mild bondage love making games, and soon have quite a dungeon like setting in their two-car garage for their kinky fun and games.

50. BONUS

51. Same scenario as number 49 only the husband confides to his brother what he and the wife do, and allows his brother to surprisingly find the dungeon, while he is away on business, and tie up his wife, and have fun with her all unknown to his wife, who does not tell her husband about her bondage session with his brother.

52. Couple places plastic sheets on floor and cover themselves with baby, and olive oil, and slide around, and have wet and slippery sex, extremely messy fun.

As noted earlier, please bear in mind that most of these story ideas, and scenarios may be changed to fit the subject matter you wish to primarily write about. They are merely tools to assist you with your creative endeavors, starting you on your way in a direction. Obviously, it is up to you to steer along the course you are seeking to write about. You can combine many of these assorted topics, and story ideas to create even more for additional sales potential. If in doubt look up legalities, so you do not break any laws with taboo erotica stories. It is not my intention to offend anyone with the various scenarios I have suggested here.

The Last Series:

1. A female who enjoys using all sorts of large, and bizarre sex toys on herself, as well as her many kinky girlfriends, see how creative you can get with some of the latex monsters, and contraptions you conjure up for her to play with

2. Two weightlifters find some fun ways to have sex in the gym, late at night after closing time.

3. A sweet young thing who seems to enjoy all well peeing on her many men friends, while having sex with them (Water sports)

4. Over sexed anal loving female who is way out of control when it comes to having anal sex performed on her nice tight buns.

5. Sex at the garbage dump, or in a dumpster, or back of a garbage truck for scent oriented sexual satisfaction

6. Loner on all girl's college team is tormented by two of her teammates, until the entire team has its way with her for complete control, and humiliation of her.

7. During long car ride your girlfriend pees her pants, and you both find out how this will add newfound ways of having sex in your already busy sex life.

8. A local photographer offers boudoir photos for Valentine's Day, only to find he ends up taking more than just photos of a few well-endowed females, who pose for him.

9. Local video club finds a new way to keep members interest, as they hire females to pose, and dance nude for the camcorders, and soon some offer solo performances.

10. A female who only enjoys having sex while inserting her big strap on inside of willing females

11. Exploits of a peep show dancer, as she exposes, and performs for the men in the tiny rooms surrounding her glass lined room where she does all sorts of lewd things.

12. Man into just legs, on women long sexy slender legs with stockings, and pantyhose covering them.

13. Female likes to ride on motorcycle behind her man, with a vibrator stuck up inside of her, the combined motion of the big throbbing bike pulsating beneath her, and her own latex invader pounding away inside of her, drive her crazy, as she speeds along the highway.

14. The tongue bather, a man who only likes to lick a woman's body everywhere, I mean everywhere, leaving no spot untouched, no matter what of where it is.

15. Male/female returns home for high school reunion, and confronts old friends, and sex partners for some hot fun, and games now that they are more select in what turns them on

sexually.

16. Maid walks in on man in hotel room, as he fists himself, and about to come, and what she does next to help him is much more than basic maid service.

17. Male/female gets jailed on purpose, just to have sex with the same sex.

18. Female babysitter seduces her boss, only it is the wife, and not the husband she is after to have hot steamy female sex with

19. Male uses laundry room in his apartment complex to get dirty female underwear, however, gets caught, and must pay the price with one female tenant who is not so understanding.

20. Two co-workers have weird sex in the back storeroom on some cardboard boxes.

21. Female asks male to fist her.

22. Hot wax and clothes pins, as mild punishment, then alligator clips to hard nipples, and hard twisted pinching

23. Older Father spies on his stepdaughter, who is in early twenties watching her change and bath, and then play with herself, as she unknowingly turns him on

24. Compulsive masturbator hires hookers, so he can masturbate in front of them, as if for them, and eventually on them, and on various areas of their naked anatomy.

25. Female dresses up as male, and goes into men's room stalls, and masturbates, as she listens to men around her going to the bathroom, or ironically doing the same thing as her.

26. A lesbian who enjoys double penetrations from her female lovers

27. Man, mistakenly picks up a transexual, yet she has big tits, she has small penis, and he decides to experiment with her to see what being with a man is like, especially since she is so small.

28. Young female catches her older male neighbor watching, as

she sunbathes topless, and punishes him by having him be her toilet slave, although it is vile, and humiliating, he soon begins to like it, and wants her to be even nastier to him for being so naughty.

29. Go to bondage store where you can hire a mistress to dominate you in one of the many back-room dungeons.

30. College coed finds out why her rent was so cheap, as the older full figured land lady comes to collect the rent due her.

31. Kinky couple come up with a wildly designed contraption on which they have sex with others.

32. Normal heterosexual couple have endless love making sessions in which they do everything imaginable to each other.

33. Eighteen-year-old videographer leaves his camcorder in closet aimed at his parent's bed, and then at his older sister's bed, and the play back reveals some hot secrets.

34. Female demands her man eat his own come, as it runs from her ass, after he has had anal sex with her.

35. Period piece of a sexual scenario, which might have taken place in war time.

36. Man enjoys having other strange men, mostly big strong and burly, pee all over him, as he kneels before them, and then see what happens next.

37. A male master who dominates females, and even trains some wayward wives for their husbands.

38. A couple who takes their vacation, by signing each other into being trained by a dominant, he by a woman, and her by a man, or so they thought.

39. Dressing totally in rubber garments, and having sex with each other, of course there are cut outs in all the appropriate areas in the garments, the smells, and sounds making for more bizarre sex.

40. My first time with a virgin. Losing one's virginity.
41. Taking a long-distance drive naked, and offering to pick up hitch hikers, and seeing which ones would accept, and/or decline your more than generous offers.
42. Having hot, and hard sex with men in uniforms
43. During Halloween party have sex with stranger, while both still disguised, and never knowing who it was even after doing some rather bizarre things with them too.
44. Working in an adult video/bookstore and talking about some of the weird things that go on each night.
45. Having sex with a parent, and their legal aged child (this can be done numerous ways from many viewpoints so work with it)
46. A person in power getting in a sticky situation, and what they are made to do to not be exposed.
47. Working on the set for a day of an adult video, and all that you see happen, and what also happens to you from it.
48. Girl that only likes guys well endowed, and how she handles them, and what some of the sizes have been, and just where they have been in her.
49. Favorite sexual positions, some normal, and some not so normal by any standards
50. Sissygasms, being transformed into a sissy by an older woman, same age woman, man, or even by yourself.
51. Sex in strange places, movie theater, public places crowded, public transportation, museums, outdoors in plain sight in day light, night, etc. etc.
52. BONUS, be sure to write down some of your own ideas that you get when reading these, so you can begin adding to the lists for yourselves. After all, even with all these examples there are so many more. These are merely to stimulate you're thinking, as an erotica writer.

Hopefully these story ideas have over stimulated you're writing senses by now, allowing you to begin your first story today. As you can see, many of these storylines can inspire others of the same, if not different story directions. It is entirely up to you, the erotica writer. As always, just make sure what you write about is legal. Legalities differ in different areas, such as states, and even countries. So, make sure to do you due diligence, and research what is legally acceptable. This will vary from publisher to publisher as well.

Chapter 17

Adult Publisher's Addresses

Newsletter List Names & addresses on this page

A.L.S. & A. A. L.
PO Box 289 Marietta, GA 30061-1289

Details
Box 4915 E 93 Main PO Vancouver, BC Canada V6B

Adventure Line Newsletter. For Adventurous Adults
PO Box 7683 Mission Hills, CA 91346-7683

Sharp Bulletins
Dept DE
PO Box 20001 Cols. Ohio 43220

Albertsen's
Box 339 Nevada City, NV 95959

The Exchange
PO Box 386 Clay/DEL 19703

Pisces
Box 207 Coloma, WI 54930

The Enamoured Writer
PO Box 451522 Sunrise, FLA 33345-15222

M W Pen Pal World
PO Box 3121 Hutchinson, KS 67501

Naughty & Nice Drexel Publishing Co.
PO Box 1514 Chicago, Ill.60690-1514

The Erotic Advertiser
Rte 1 Box 262 Talbotton, GA 31827

Chit-Chat Newsletter B&B Management
PO Box 2372 Elizabethtown, KY 42792

CIS, Inc Tidewater Blue
POB 9645 Norfolk, VA23505-0645

Alternative
POB 45112 Little Rock, AR 72214

New Fantasy Penmate Club
PO Box 1353 Imperial Beach, CA 91933-1353

J. Harshman
POB 336 Angola, IN 46703

Searchlit Publications GPO
Box 2775 New York, NY 10116-2775

SWANK Publications Inc. Editorial Offices

210 Route 4 East Suite 401 Paramus, New Jersey
07652-5116

Wade Inc.
Box 69 Junction City, Oregon 97448

Infantae Press
PO Box 1246 Seattle, WA 96111

Assorted Foot Nacs B & D Company
4501 Van Nuys Blvd. Suite 215 Sherman Oaks, CA 91403

Libido
5318 N. Paulina Street Chicago, IL 60640

Platinum
4501 Van Nuys Blvd. Suite 215 Sherman Oaks, CA 91403

Drake Publishers, Inc.
801 2nd Avenue New York, New York 10017-4776

Panty Line Fever Rick Inc.
27 Avenue C Apt. 3D New York, N. Y. 10009-7849

Playboy Enterprises
919 N. Michigan Ave Chicago, IL 60611

Midlife Publications
462 Broadway New York, New York 10013

The Enamored Writer
PO Box 634945 Margate, FLA 33063

Paramour Magazine
PO Box 949 Cambridge, MA 02140-0008

Aereola
PO Box 3611 San Diego, CA 92163

The Home Front
426 East North Street Suite 32 Wakesha, WI 53188

AVN Publications
6700 Valjean Ave Van Nuys, CA 91406

Diaper Pail Friends
38 Miller Avenue Suite 127 Mill Valley, CA 94941

Retro Systems "WHAP"
1850 Union Street #1261 San Francisco, CA 94123

The Write Solution
Flat 1 11 Holland Road
Hove, Susex BN3 1JF England

Polo Productions
100 Brunnell Street #4B Anchorage, AK 99508-5819

Cavalier
2355 Salzedo St Coral Gables, FL 33134

Best American Erotic Stories
309 Cedar St #3-D Santa Cruz, CA 95060

EROS
351 West 54th St New York, New York 10019

Yellow Silk-Journal of Erotic Arts
Box 6374 Albany, New York 94706

American Art Ent.
Box 1368 Sun Valley, CA 91353-1368

Titan Books
4244 Dolbern ST London SE1 OU

Adam Film World Knight Pubs
8060 Melrose Ave Los Angeles, CA 90046

Fling-Relim Pubs
550 Miler Ave Mill Valley, CA 94941

Video View

POB 15608 North Hollywood, CA 91615

Ambience
POB 12134 Berkeley, CA 94712

Taste of Latex
POB 35010 Phoenix, AZ 85069-5010

Eidos
POB 96 Boston, MA 62137

Gallery-Montcalm Pub
401 Park Ave South New York, N.Y. 10016-8802

Brat Attack
POB 40754 San Francisco, CA 94140-0754

Hot Male Review/Magcorp
801 Second Ave New York, New York 10013

Leg Glamour/Juggs
462 Broadway 4th Flr. New York, New York, 10013

Gent
14411 Commerce Way Ste 420 Miami Lakes, FL 33016-1598

Forum
1965 Broadway New York, New York 10023

Drummer/Machcorp Dsesmondus Inc
24 Sotwell St San Francisco, CA 94103

Virgin Pubs/London Bridge
854 River Dock Dr Ste 202 Buffalo, New York 14207

Magcorp/Small Tops
POB 801434 Santa Clarita, CA 91380-1434

C. F. Pubs
Box 706 East Setauket, New York 11733

Slippery When Wet
POB 348 New York, New York 10009

Blue Moon Books
61 Fourth Ave New York, New York 10003

Penthouse
277 Park Ave 4th Floor New York, New York 10172

Leg Tease
POB 584 Amityville, New York 11701

Permeable Press
#4 47Noe ST San Francisco, CA 94114-1017

Porno Pen /Black Book
POB 31155 San Francisco, CA 94131

Mavety
462 Broadway Ste: 4000 New York, New York 10013

Leg Show
155 Avenue of the Americas New York, New York 10013

Leg Scene/Paradise Magazine
Ste: 2208 350 Fifth St New York, New York 10018

Obelesk Books
POB 1118 Elkton, MD 21922-1118

High Society
801 Second Ave New York, New York 10013

Outbound Press
89 Fifth Ave. Ste: 303 New York, N.Y. 10003-1630

Gentleman's Companion Hudson Comm.
155 Avenue of the Americas New York, New York 10013

Brush Creek Media
2215 R Market St #148 San Francisco, CA 94114

Dugent Publishing Corp.

14411 Commerce Way Suite 420 Miami Lakes, FLA 33016-1598

Rocky Mountain Oyster/Tabloid

PO Box 27467 Denver, CO 80227

Masquerade/Books

801 Second Avenue New York, New York 10017

BOOK FORMAT PUBLISHERS Names & Addresses below are for full length book publishers...

CATALOGUES Many of companies below contain Names & Addresses of catalogues...

DIRECTORIES AVAILABLE which contain numerous publications... Query for prices, they are excellent resources.

You will notice since this list is old, and just how many erotica-oriented businesses thrived well before the internet. Now that many no longer exist, at least with the internet browsing and searching/researching for them is much much easier now, with immediate results.

Blue Moon Books

61 Fourth Avenue New York, New York 10003

Roni Raye Productions

PO Box 502210 Indianapolis, IN 46250

Creative Arts Book Company
833 Bancroft Way Berkeley, CA 94710

TLC
POB 10 Costilla, NM 87524

Albertsen's 1,000 Worldwide Contact Clubs
PO Box 339 Nevada City, NV 95959

Carlyle Communications LTD Beeline Books
462 Broadway Suite 4000 New York, New York 10013

Intimate Treasures/Love Stuff
POB 77902 San Francisco, CA 94107-0902

Adult Directory NPAA
PO Box 120768 East Haven, CT 06512

Star Distributors
PO Box 362. Canal Street Station New York, N. Y. 10013

Worldwide Intimates
POB 468 Burbank, CA 91503

Pleasure Plays
1416 Court Chariton, Iowa 50049

Nexus Erotic Fiction Virgin Publishing Company
332 Ladbroke Grove London W10 5AH

Catalogs Worldwide Interstate Enterprises
PO Drawer 19689 Houston, TX 77224

The Black Book
PO Box 31155-A96 San Francisco, CA 94131

NASCA Lifestyles Press
2641 W. La Palma #A Anaheim, CA 92801-2602

Adam & Eve PHE, Inc.
POB 800 Carrboro, NC 27510

Newsletter   Editorial   Resource   Direct   Marketing
Association
11 West 42nd Street 25th Floor New York, New York
10030-8096

Carroll & Graf Publishers, Inc.
260 Fifth Ave New York, New York 10001

Permeable Press
#4 47 Roe St San Francisco, CA 94114-1017

Pocket Books
1230 Avenue of the Americas New York, New York 10020

LIBIDO The Journal of Sex & Sensibility
PO Box 146721 Chicago, IL 60614

Mixed Media Enterprises
501 East 87th Street Suite 9C New York, New York 10128

Firsthand LTD
PO Box 1314 Teaneck, New Jersey 07666

In Step
PO Box 386 Walnut, CA 91788

Artemis Creations Publishing
3395 Nostrand Avenue #2-J Brooklyn, New York 11229

FOX Magazine Montcalm Publishing Corp.
401 Park Avenue South New York, New York 10016-8807

Quad International
214 West Grant Tucson, AZ 85705

DM International
PO Box 35010 Phoenix, AZ 85069-5010

Executive Imports
PO Box 1839 New York, New York 10016-1839

Sunshine Publishing Company, Inc. Hotshots
7060 Convoy Court San Diego, CA 92111

Letters Magazine
PO Box 1314 Teaneck, New Jersey 07666

Bon-Vue Enterprises, Inc.
901 West Victoria Street Unit "G" Compton, CA 90220

LFP Inc./HG Publications Hustler/Hustler Busty Beauties
8464 Wilshire Blvd Ste: 900 Beverly Hills, CA 90211

Contact Advertising
POB 3431 Fort Pierce, FLA 34948

Players
8060 Melrose Avenue Los Angeles, CA 90046

AJA/Sportmatic
PO Box 470 Port Chester, New York 10573

New Esoteric Press
Box 300689 JFK Station Jamaica, New York 11430-0689

Playgirl
801 Second Avenue New York, New York 10017

Penthouse International LTD. General Media Publishing
Corp.
277 Park Ave 4th Floor New York, New York 10172

Winter Publications Co.
Box 80667 South Dartmouth, MA 02748

Networx Homemade Hot Shots
Box 3323 Springfield, MA 01101

Eton Publishing/Vanity
1775 Broadway Suite 604 New York, New York
10019-1903

SHE
Box 637 Capitola, CA 95010

Turn Ons
313 West 53rd Street New York, New York 10019

Milky Way Productions Inc.
43 West 24th Street New York, New York 10010

Video Xcitement
Box 187 Fraser, MI 48026

TV/TS Chronicles
855 E. Twain Suite #123-547 Las Vegas, NV 89109

Chapter 18

Pen Pal Groups

Pen Pal Groups

Simmons Company
POB 880761 San Francisco, CA 94188

Erotic Penpals
POB 919 Inglis, FLA 34449-0919

SIGNAL INTERNATIONAL
Box 150 F1-15111 Lahti, Finland

Friendship Express
POB 581515 Minneapolis, MN 55458

Ekkehard Lory
POB 1209 9001 St. Gallen Switzerland (enclose 1RC)

Exotic Pen Pals MPC
1222 Hazel Street North St. Paul, MN 55119-4500

Worldwide Pen Pal Club
1805 Sunset Road SE Rio Rancho, NM 87124

Romantic Pen Pals
POB 2481 St. Louis, MO 63114

David Dunn Correspondence Club
Suite 627 1626 N. Wilcox Ave. Hollywood, CA 90028-6206

Details
Box 4915 E93 Main PO Vancouver, BC Canada V6B 4A6

New Fantasy Penmate Club
POB 1353 Imperial Beach, CA 91933-1353

The Mail Exchange
POB 1277 Lompoc, CA 93438-1277

Friends with Pens
POB 6410 Denver, CO 80206

Intl Pen Friends
POB 516071 Dallas, TX 75251-6071

Kate's Connections
2554 Lincoln Blvd. #112 Marina Del Rey, CA 90291

Letter Writers Sheet
POB 2201 Bartow, FLA 33830

MW PenPal World Magazine
POB 48193 Wichita, KS 67201-8193

Worldwide Pen Adv/Indio Society
31 Olive Road Ocala, FLA 32672

Start a Pen Pal Club. Send SASE and $ 1.00 to:
R&R Enterprises
PO Box 416 Wilton, Iowa 52778

INTRODUCTION GROUPS

Albertsen's 1000 Worldwide Contact Clubs
POB 339 Nevada City, NV 95959

Alternative Lifestyles Directory 97
POB 80667 South Dartmouth, MA 02748

Secrets Magazine
Box 70 Gover Road ST Austell PL25 5NG England
The Singles Exchange
Box 232 Deer Park, New York 11729

Opportunities Unlimited
POB 20512 Sarasota, FLA 34276

Veronica's Secrets
1410 Goode Midland, TX 79701

Roni Raye Productions (Catalog)
POB 502210 Indianapolis, IN 46250

N & N Encounters Club
POB 6531 Champaign, IL 61826

Telstar Intl
POB 66 Kington, Herefordshire HR5 3YA UK

Sharp Bulletins
Dept DE POB 2002 Col', OHIO 43220

BBW Express
POB 16988 North Hollywood, CA 91615

Hot Connections/Single Tymes
POB 270726 Corpus Christi, TX 78427

Exotic introductions
POB 418 Williamson, New York 14589

Flaming Desire
POB 601454 San Jose, CA 95161

Globe Collectors & Traders Club
3941 Pacific Blvd. San Mateo, CA 94437

Writers Exchange/S.L. Ghivan
4432 W. Maypole Chicago, IL 60624

500 Girls Intl.
POB 7688 2000 Hamburg, 19, Germany

Signal Intl
Box 150 FI-15111 Lahti, Finland ($ 1.00 or 2 IRC's)

NEWSLETTERS

Chit Chat Newsletter B&B Mngmt
POB 2373 Elizabethtown, KY 42702

Newsletter Editorial Resource
11 West 42nd Street 25th Floor New York, New York
10030-8096

Loving Alternatives Magazine
POB 459 San Dimas, CA 91733

Singles Connection
POB 22 Aiken, SC 29802-0022

Singles Magazine/Homestead Hotline
720 Morrow Ave Clayton, New Jersey 08312-2102

Key Press FAR OUT
POB 26048 El Paso, TX 79926

Silver Nugget Fdn. Dept SK
907 River Rd #129 Eugene, OR 97404

Paxius Happy Viking
Box 23009 S-200 45 Malimo, Sweden

Multi Club Magazine
Prenzel/Kuebler Ring 44 63834 Sulzbach/Main/Germany

Pisces
Box 207 Coloma, WI 54930

Adventure Line Newsletter
POB 7683 Mission Hills, CA 91346-7683

Swingset J&S Unlimited Inc.
POB 811 Osprey, FLA 34229

Meet People
POB 247 Osseo, MN 55369

Rocky Mtn Oyster
POB 27467 Denver, CO 80227

Singles RSVP
POB 14567 Las Vegas, NV 89114

International Exchange
Verboorstr.35, Bus 8, 8380 Zeebbrugge Belgium

Bent Bay/Beat Post/Sweet Dane
POB 37 880 Viborg, Denmark

Meetings Italia c/o: Lisbeth Lundqvist
Via del Orinolo 23 50122 Firenze, Italy

Chapter 19

Websites Pertaining to Writing Erotica & Stories

porncorner.com
  sexsense.com
  sabrina.org
  planetmojo.com
  lierotica.com
  best.com (laura w spanking stories)
  joanelloyd.com (jlmain)
  voyeurismstories.com
  storylist.com
  adult-stories.com
  accelnet.com (victoria stories)
  slowhand.com (ezone)
  annejet.pair.com
  adultfiction.com. (main)
  hersalon.com
  her-erotica.com
  missouri.edu. (writer/writer)
  harbour.sfu.ca (ccsp citation net writers)
  cris.com. (tooshoes. PenPartners)
  pinkflamingo.com
  erotica-readers.com. (ERA)
  red-light.porncity.net. (146. More)
  xxxploration.com
  very-koi.net
  very-koi.net (works erotic erotica)
  members.tripod.com (MrErotic. Index)
  tpe.com

tpe.com (mule write tips)

qz.to (eli erotica assm)

qz.to (Erotica assm wiindex)

escape.com

members.aol.com. (healwell sex)

escape.com. (sbw story)

escape.com (story ssgalore)

netscape.com. (browsers create sites)

dreamscape.com. (stories)

1819.com. (stories)

sexnsexy.com (stories)

thewebspider.com (over 18 nancy stories)

richards-realm.com. (choice)

cws.internet.com (32 menu)

newslettersonly.com

gpforums.com

woods.bianca.com. (shacklet White_Shadow)

iam.com. (maryanne)

users.lanminds.com. (mohanraj Home)

sex.funfun.net

immoralsex.com. (sexstories. Main)

nifty.org. (nifty)

sexplosion2.com. (main)

pub.savvy.com

cleansheets.com

webcom.com. (impulse list)

11.pai.com. (Julie main)

Winnipeg.freenet.mb.ca

dspace.dial.pipex.com (town square 177 stories)

sabrina.org

iam.com

akula.com. (zigzag dirty)

JoanELloyd.com. (jillinks)
gaycafe.com
compsinc.com
xxxgroup.com
elite.net. (natasha)
xxxpen.holowww.com
cybertron.com
omen.com.au
monkey.hooked.net
netaxis.com. (mike30061 links)
home.clara.net (darkwanderer home)
members.aol.com. (Avon747. Index)
goecities.com. (WestHollywood 6027 exhibitionism)
cord.iupui.edu
yahoo.com (News & Media Magazines Sex Women)
arcticera.com (stories)
nifty.org
members.tripod.com
xanadu2000.freeserve.co.uk
darkmall.com
eccentrica.org. (eryssa index)
members.aol.com (UpTaaCamp private alter index)
tpe.com. (mule)
members.triod.com. (MrErotic index)
peacockblue.com
madeline-sex.com
porncorner.com. (members my erotica. Index)
spraycan.sincware.com
young-stuff.com. (frank)

Chapter 20

Writing Erotica for Fun & Profit Revised Edition

As I mentioned in the introduction, the book is divided into two sections. The first being the original 19-chapter edition, written years ago, when there were no digital eBooks and/or self-publishing houses. So, of course a good amount of the original material in this book is obsolete, with many of the links, and contact resources, no longer in business. This will give you an idea of just how far the erotica market has changed over the years, much like adult websites.

Notice, there are no longer as many adult men's magazines on the newsstands, not as many adult videos, and bookstores. Now everyone has the internet located right inside their homes. One thing is certain, is that it does make it easier to purchase erotica, and read on your cell phone, tablet, or computer. These technological gadgets have become the new versions of the adult book, magazine, and video stores, where erotica publications originated years ago.

So, the following chapters will all be the Revised Edition, which will take you into the digital age of publishing. Fortunately, for you is that this new age makes erotica writing much easier, however much more competitive.

Do not despair, there is always a market for erotica. You simply must choose what kinky niche and/or niches you want to write about. Just remember to always keep your erotica writing legal. Do your due diligence in research. Of course, what is illegal in one area, might be legal in another. Just as some self-publishers are stricter than others when it comes to your writing, and the images used on your cover, as well as within your book.

Fortunately, you can navigate around these due to numerous self-publishing, and sales companies, and websites. You decide what you want to write, and how to publish, and market it for sales. I am on several social media pages, and have my own website, bbpierceauthor (dot) com and email bbpierceauthor@yahoo.com to be contacted at. Anytime any of you reading this have any questions, please feel free to contact me with them. I will be happy to answer any of them that I am able to.

Use social media to reach out to other erotica writers. I have met so many wonderful talented writers online in social media. I am on Facebook, and Twitter under bbpierceauthor.

So, you just must read what you feel as an aspiring erotica writer, or perhaps a seasoned one just looking for something you may have overlooked. Sadly, many of the addresses. and websites are no longer in operation. The good news is that there are tons of new ones.

Writing on a computer is a breeze now. You have auto spell correct, software for just about anything to make writing easier for you. There are even audio software programs allowing you to dictate your work. One thing that I must mention is you, and only you will be responsible for doing some of the research yourself. I cannot mention all the available writing software and hardware tools, or even rate them in here for you. The same goes for publishing platforms, and marketing arenas. You will need to do this, so dust off whatever search engine you use, and do YOUR own due diligence. Today there is so much out there to help writers.

Chapters 21 through 52 are all new and comprise the revised portion of the book. What I am doing is bringing you into the digital age of erotica writing, even though you are already here. Although it may seem easier to write erotica today, as compared to earlier days, it simply means what we have as tools, and avenues. The real difficulty, as it has always been, is writing. Today with all the advantages the digital age affords writers, at the same time it offers so many more distractions. These can be a writer's Achilles heel. Time, and the wasting of it.

Previously, a telephone might ring, or a television might be playing to distract you, yet never you're writing devices. Now on your computer you have so many temptations to distract you from writing, it is amazing. Many of us wear a telephone on our wrists. So, it is much, much easier for all of us too slowly leave our writing zone. You cannot, just stay strong, and do not be tempted, unless you do suffer writer's block. Then take that break, utilize that distraction, whatever is necessary for you to regain yourself into your writing zone.

I am also offering my erotica writing expertise to all your 18+ with any questions about writing erotica. Simply Dm, Message, or email me bbpierceauthor@yahoo.com Visit my website bbpierceauthor (dot) com.

Once you have your own erotica writer website, I invite you to trade links with me. All you must do is ask.

So now sit back and enjoy the read. I suggest you keep a notebook nearby to jot down notes, and ideas in, as they come to mind during your reading of this book. This is especially a good idea to have by your bed in the event you get an erotica story idea late at night. Just write it down so you have it in your notes for the future. I always keep it near my computer when writing. Maybe a personal recorder would be better for you.

Remember all you must do is START WRITING EROTICA, no excuses, just results. Stay safe. However, before you start writing, please finish reading this book. You are about to start the Revised Edition section, so enjoy, and remember YOU can contact me with any questions at any time, so you are never alone in your writing erotica adventure. So, get comfortable, and let's get started.

Chapter 21: Stationary, Letterheads, & Envelopes

Currently, you can still use stationary, letterheads, and envelopes, however, most publishers do not request, nor require them. The beauty of submitting your work via the internet is the ease, and speed that it offers you, plus the savings of postage that would be required if mailing it.

I must mention that although I am using the same subject matter, as far as chapters from the earlier edition of this book, I will be updating areas when, and where I can. This is just so you can see what has changed, and what has not, plus some areas that may be during changing. New information will be added so that you can see what changes have and are taking place in the erotica writing industry. Some chapters will be much larger than others. I just wanted to let you know this, as we continue our erotica writer journey.

For instance, I no longer utilize paper, mainly because I do not submit my work anymore. There are so many outlets to self-publish your work. Currently, I am using Amazon Kindle Unlimited to self-publish my stories, in eBook form. They also allow you to self-publish in paperback, whereby the formatting is slightly different, as is the size of the book cover. This does not mean you have to do what I do. If you wish to use paper, I am sure there are publishers that will allow it. You just need to research it.

You can offer short stories, and novels of all lengths. Previously I used to group my stories of a certain erotica niche to make a bigger book, and charge more for it. Then, I realized I could just sell individual stories cheaper, yet sell them individually. It just means more work, as far as formatting your work, adding it into their program, and designing a book cover, of course you can pay others to do all of this for you. Right now, I am contemplating bundling my shorter stories of the same kinky niche back into longer books to market as paperbacks. Again, I am still in the research mode with this. See, research never ends for writers, so please be sure to enjoy it, otherwise you could become easily frustrated by it.

It just depends on how much you are willing to pay. After all you can pay to promote your work by placing paid advertising or utilizing the services of a professional promotion company. I find when you are just beginning you do not have the extra needed funds to pay for this. Although every erotica writer is different, so perhaps you can afford to spend money on your erotica writing, even before you make any from it.

I will cover more of this further in this section of the book. Let me remind you to take notes along the way, as you read this, in the event you have any questions you wish to submit to me. My contact information is inserted throughout this book to make it easier to find it. bbpierceauthor@yahoo.com

Chapter 22: Handwritten Versus Typed

Obviously, many of you may still not have a word processor/computer/tablet, etc. I suggest you query to find them to use without paying for it if necessary. I personally still jot down notes, and story ideas, and titles by hand. Later, I transfer them into my computer. A computer allows you to make any changes so much easier, not to mention storing all your work, and research.

In the event you still wish to hand write your erotica stories, you always can have someone else input it into a computer, or even to type it out on a typewriter. You can also dictate it if you wish.

So, if you can use a computer, whenever you write erotica, I suggest that you do so. Again, this is entirely up to you. I use a MacBook Air, and used to use a MacBook Pro previously, and found I did not need that much power for writing and design. All I am trying to explain is the ease that the computer affords you, especially if you are thinking of designing your own book covers. I use my iPad to read erotica for research, and then write my reviews by hand to later send via computer to the authors. Later in this book, I will delve into reviewing erotica, which is something I am quite anal about. After all, if you can read erotica, you can review it. Just remember that, as erotica writers. Reading the work of other writers allows you research and opens your mind to all sorts of erotica subjects, and story ideas. After all, you never know just where you might get your next story idea from.

Simply reviewing erotica, we all help the writers to improve, if and where needed. It can inform a writer about just what sorts of stories the readers want more of to read, which increases sales, and income. There is no need to get into too much detail, or to become brutal in our reviews. Give them kudos when earned, and a few helpful hints where the story may be lacking, for you, as an erotica reader.

So, as you can see it is perfectly fine to either writer or type. Work with what is best for you when writing erotica. After all you are the erotica writer.

Chapter 23: Query Letters

Today, query letters are not used as much. I say this because I do not want to ever discourage any new erotica writers from asking editors what sort of work they need. Naturally today, query letters can be submitted via email on a computer, rather than hard copies on paper, sent in envelopes, via USPS. So, as you can see, some things change, while others do not. The changes you see here have mostly been made by me as well. As the writing industry changes, so must the writers.

There are also websites for publications, and some geared to erotica writers that list current needs for articles, stories, etc. Others run contests you can enter. There are some seeking works to be included in anthologies of specific story niches. Again, you the erotica writer must do your due diligence, and research on this. These websites will be listed further along in the book. Always remember what I list in here I am not standing behind, just showing you what pops up when you research it. Be aware new websites are always popping up, and many are leaving. Just keep your finger on the pulse of the market and check regularly by researching it.

Chapter 24: Writer's Guidelines

Normally, I would think that no matter what erotica publisher you find they will have some sort of writer's guidelines to adhere too, and many will be different. So be ready to be adaptive to each one. So here is an area from the original book that has not changed. So now, instead of printing them out to keep on file, you can create a digital file for that publisher on your computer.

Plus, once you have individual files for publishing houses/ publishers that you want to submit to, you can then keep a file of your submitted stories/articles to them. Erotica writers can write stories, books, articles, interviews, reviews, and anything else a publisher might be seeking. What you write about is up to you. There are even free websites you can have your work read on. These do not offer you any monetary compensation, just a platform to gather fans from. You might consider starting out doing this, however, I like to make money with my work. I might not sell the story immediately, yet if it is in my library on Amazon, and soon elsewhere, as well, I have the potential to make a sale 24/7, and internationally.

This is where social media groups, and writer forums come into play. Joining the ones, you like and become part of the commentary. You will meet others who have questions that need answers, and some can give you recommendations, and even reviews on things that you might be considering purchasing. These are places that you can gain valuable information. Learning from others and helping them learn from you is important. Always learn from other's mistakes, whenever you can. Sometimes it beats learning from your own. At least it can be less painful for you.

Chapter 25: Margin Guidelines

When you use writing software, you can use what they have dialed in already. Unless you want a specific margin, then you can be creative. I always use what Pages on MacBook offers me, by default. I have used Word in the past and export to it when formatting my work for self-publishing websites.

Now in this new age of erotica writing, where margins do come into play, is during book cover design for paperbacks since they all vary in size. To be honest, I design all my own book covers for my eBooks and have yet to publish any paperbacks. I do plan on this soon, and know it is an entirely different design process, and you must add your own margins etc. So, this will be another learning curve for me. Of course, this is another challenge that I am up for. Book cover design will be covered later in this section of the book.

Always bear in mind, as you read the material in this book, that it is my version, and my experiences. These are avenues I have chosen to go down. You may agree, or disagree, whichever you chose. The fact that I did not utilize a specific tool, or way of doing things, does not mean you should not also, or vice versa. I just want you to know what is available for you out there, and always emphasize you to research all you can, as fully as you can. Always do your due diligence, and get professional advice, when, and where needed.

Chapter 26: Synopsis Example

As always, a synopsis is a synopsis. Just be sure to follow each writer guideline you are submitting your work to. They might want a synopsis to be different than what I suggest, or even from others you have submitted already.

Just follow what the publisher/editor requests, and you will be fine.

Within the file you create for that publisher, you might make note if there are any synopsis differences then what you are used to using. If so, then simply make the necessary adjustment to yours to meet their standards.

Not much else to say about this since it is pretty much self-explanatory.

Chapter 27: Research

Research will always be research, and there is no getting around it. If you are unfamiliar with something, research it. Goggle, and other search engines make our lives so much easier now. So just go with the flow. After all research is, as research does. You obtain the needed answers to your questions, solutions to your problems, etc.

For instance, you can research publishers online to find out who is looking for what sort of erotica. This can be book publishers, magazines, websites, and every avenue where you can sell your writing.

Now suppose you want to get creative, and write erotica about a kinky niche that you are not that familiar, or sexually experienced with? You can research it to the point that when you write about it, no readers will even think that you are not an expert in the field. Research can be as simple as reading erotica by other authors, especially the best-selling ones. What about watching adult videos for specific sexual acts? It will allow you to describe them in much more vivid detail. I have even researched what bondage rooms looked like, and all the various BDSM apparatus that is involved, so I could describe the rooms in my stories in more debauched detail. So, as you can now see, research is your friend. Always utilize it to your best advantage.

As you begin you might want to know the length of a short story, to see for a specific amount to charge for it. Just research it. Again, is for self-publishing because most publishing houses will set your price for you. Remember every self-publishing writer sells their work for what they feel will make it sell best. So just because another erotica writer sells all their stories for $ 0.99. does not mean that you must. Always test the waters, because you can always change your prices until you see which dollar amount pricing sell the most. You can always offer sales when you wish if you are self-publishing.

Research is also about reading the #1 Erotica Bestselling Authors' works. This allows you to see what is selling the most, and why. Another avenue is researching hot selling kinky niches. There is no sense spending the time to write n erotica story if that kinky niche I not welling well. Then there is keyword research, to show you what are the best keywords to use in a specific kinky niche book. Keywords are also very important for SEO.

Although research may be time consuming, it is always time well spent, especially when the results help you to write an erotica book that readers want to buy and then just how to promote it using the right keywords. Yes, this chapter might be a bit vague, yet I have given you all the pertinent subject matter. Now it is up to you to do your research on it even further so that you understand it completely.

Any questions you have about writing erotica, or writing in general, can all be answered by research. So, get used to it. I suggest you read all the books about writing erotica and writing in general and take what information you need from each one of them, because I do not think that there is one book with all the answers you seek and need.

Just as I mention about various writing products and tools. You must decide which one's work for you the best, and then review them to make sure they are worth it.

My goal here is to give you the confidence to begin writing erotica. You might want to do it for fun, or just to know that some horny stranger is reading your work and masturbating to it somewhere in the world. Maybe you do want to make some extra inCOME from it and sell your work. Whatever the reason I hope this book will get you started and on your way into the world of erotica writing.

Now can YOU see all the possibilities that research has to offer you? Oh, and sometimes you even must research your research.

Chapter 28: Reference Material

This can now fall into the same category as research. Although there are still hard copy books, and magazines you can refer to, yet it is research. Suppose you are considering purchasing some new writing software, you would want to read reviews on it, right? This is researching, because you are reading the reference material for it in the form of reviews.

Reference material can also fall under the category of resource material. How to books on writing, thesauruses, dictionaries, writer's guidelines, and more, all are reference materials to any writer. Just as you are reading this publication on writing erotica, I seriously urge you to read those written by other authors. You might gain just one piece of important information that helps you, and that is all you need. Much of it you can also find online and in software you can download, although some you might have to pay for.

With the internet, researching could not be easier. I know I use YOUTUBE for DIY, yet I never checked to see what they have to offer, if anything, about erotica writing. Guess what? I just did, and they have a lot of videos about erotica writing. Isn't the internet just wonderful that way? See that, I just did some research for you.

So now, as you can see, the internet makes it much easier to find answers to questions for just about anything. Just do not let too much "research" take you away from your erotica writing. Much of this will have to do with what I mentioned about watching adult videos for specific research reasons.

Chapter 29: Creating A Story Line

Previously I gave you about 250 FREE story lines to further develop, and use. Now I will add several more for you, that, as I reread the original, I found more that I now use, which I may not have utilized then. Plus, new decades bring new story ideas. Just imagine Covid-19, Uber/Lift, delivery of groceries, and home shopping items door to door? Now you know all those other story line ideas I gave you. Well, what if you rewrote them around what I mentioned in the previous line?

You can see these latest reasons for a particular storyline. Think about major events that happen internationally. Sporting events, and championships, trends of all kinds, vacations, newly developed resorts, government/political events, breaking news stories, etc. If your mind is creative, as it should be if you want to be a writer, then there is no end to the erotica you can write about. I have files and files of story ideas, and titles that I can write a story about. Hopefully, in time you will have them as well. There will be another list further along in the book.

Now don't worry, I have more of them for you to list, just nowhere as many, because you should be able to take all the ones that I gave you and add just about the same number of new ones, if not more to give you a grand total of over 500 storylines to start creating stories about and making added income with. I used added income, want to know why?

Writing erotica and selling it can make you additional income. Sales will start slow, and you should never quit your day job. It is a wonderful added income if you are retired, and a great fun filled past time. Yes, there are erotica writers that write erotica for a living. This is another research job for you. Find out who they are, and how they do it. I will cover this in more detail later. One thing you should remember about sales, and income dollar amounts, is that paid advertising might be involved. Often someone making $5000 a month, is also spending

$2000 a month, if not more to make those sales. So, in hindsight they are spending $3000 to make a profit of $2000. I just wanted you to be aware of this, especially when they show you copies of checks, just so you are not disillusioned. Just remember, the more you write, the more you must sell. The more you sell, the more money you make.

So most important is writing, just keep writing, and selling your work. There is always safety in numbers, and when it comes to writing, the higher the numbers the better. By this I mean, the more stories you have available for sale, the better the chances of making more money. Of course, you must offer sellable writing, and quite often this takes time, trial, and error. Just stay true to yourself, as a writer, and just keep writing. Along the way you will want to learn as much about writing, as you possibly can.

I have listed more storylines for you in another chapter further along in this book. Although since you are already an erotica writer, you should have some already planned in your mind. Now keep in mind, that with one storyline you always have the option to change it out. For instance, you have a storyline about a man and a woman. Now think how many different stories you can create from this one story. What I mean by this, is that you can have it as a woman and woman, a man, and a man, one woman and two men, one man and two men. Then you can write about transgendered characters.

Plus, many write about fantasy and horror, monster and alien, characters also. Just imagine the potential you have with one story and how many ways you can change and/or redirect it to suit the characters, and your readers, depending on what they desire. One story can be written so many ways. If you are new to erotica writing you still must have some idea of just what you wanted to write erotica about, as far as a kinky niche.

Just remember when you read all the ones, I have listed in here for you, that you should be able to double that number of ideas on a good

day, because "A DIRTY MIND is a terrible thing to waste, especially i
it is yours."

Chapter 30: Description & Mood

No matter what year you are writing erotica in, description and mood should never change. It is you, the erotica writer, that sets the mood/tone, and description of the story/book/article that you are writing. This is where you have complete artistic licensing. Just remember to always keep it legal, legal, and legal.

As for myself I tend to write more with sexually graphic sex scenes, while other erotica writers might not. Description and mood are both double edged swords. You want to be descriptive enough to set a mood, yet not overdo it. Always allow your readers to create as much of it in their minds as they choose to. Like they say, sometimes less is more.

BTW some of the subject matter that I am going over in this section, are answers to questions asked to me online. I had put the word out about any newbie erotica writers with questions to contact me with them, just so I could make sure that they were covered in this book. Many were however, several were not. So, this is also a way that reviewers can help writers, just as these other writers helped me to make this book more informative. For that I thank them, they know who they are.

This is why I always suggest for erotica writers to read the works of other erotica writers, especially in the same kinky niches that they intend to write in. This way you can see, firsthand what works and what does not work for readers. Plus, you can review that erotica writers work and perhaps make some new friends online. The is why I always join writing groups to post in and respond to other posts. It is a subtle way to get your name out there, and help others at times, and sometimes have them help you.

Description of your finished work is just as important for browsers to read a brief description of what your book is about. Do not make it too lengthy, just offer enough to hook them in and want more from reading it.

Bear in mind that the more you write the better you will become at these. So just keep writing, as often as you can. I cannot emphasize this enough. The more you write the more material you will have to sell. Just start with a short story.

As you progress as an erotica writer, you might find that one day you wish to crossover too romance writing, or even write erotica, and romance fiction at the same time. You might even wish to write nonfiction articles for publications which deal with the adult entertainment industry, who knows. The more you begin to see just how big erotica writing can be, is when you can make decisions about just what it is that you want to write about. Believe me, it does not have to be all about fiction. You can research positions in the adult entertainment industry, which means jobs, not actual sexual positions. Writing jobs are everywhere.

Chapter 31: Dealing with Writer's Block

WRITER'S BLOCK, what is it? I tell writers that it is simply an occupational hazard for writers. Many writers have different opinions of it, as for myself, I have experienced it many times throughout my writing career. It COMEs with the territory, much like COMING, comes with erotica, and you just must figure the way for you to best deal with it, and overcome it.

I have read so many questions about writer's block in writer's forums, and writers' groups. Yes, this never ever changes, or goes away. So, get used to it. Not to worry, all you need to do is change gears, take a break, or even begin writing another story that you cannot get out of your head, and stopped you from being able to write about another one, thus the writer's block you got.

I always have several stories going at the same time, WIP, works in progress. For some this can be confusing, for me it is just natural to have all kinds of erotica ideas and works in motion. You can do something completely difference to help clear your mind.

Also, if you are like me, and have tons of files about erotica stories, story titles, book cover designs, then you can work on these. Sometimes, when I have several stories going at once, I just switch over to resume writing on another one. However, if you are suffering from sudden erotica story burnout, then, stop writing completely.

Sometimes I just stop and do something completely different. Other times, as I have mentioned, I just stop, and switch gears with some of my notes, and files pertaining to erotica writing stories, ideas, books titles, and book cover designs. As I mentioned, I always have all sorts of notes, and ideas to draw from, and so should you. At times, I just begin to continue writing another story, which is not yet finished. Sometimes your head is into erotica, just not the subject you have writer's block for. Besides that, you can always add to stories you are working on to lengthen them, or perhaps introduce other character, or sex scene.

Once you feel the need to begin writing that same erotica story again, then do it. Meanwhile, do whatever you must, to keep your sanity when it comes to erotica writing. I know there is no such thing, as too much sex, yet at times there can be such a thing as too much erotica writing. So just pace yourself.

You may also wish to read erotica written by another erotica author. This way instead of writing it you are reading it. And remember, reading erotica is research, so at least you are still working. Thus, no guilt trips to take.

You may wish to research "Writer's Block". You will be amazed at all the reasons that they say might cause it. Just remember that we are all different, so what effects one writer may not affect you, and vice versa.

As erotica writers suffering from Writer's Block, you just must deal with and control it in whichever way works best for you. You must take control over it, and never let it get the best of you. For those of you wishing more answers about this, I suggest that you join several writers' groups, and forums online. Within these you can ask questions and compare experiences with other writers. I belong to a great number of them, mostly on Facebook. You can also find many that will allow you to promote your published books for sale. Stay strong and persevere through it, you will find that it eventually ends.

Fortunately, most of you reading this are not writing as your sole occupation. So, writer's block will just be a loss of writing time, not income, meanwhile you have another lucrative avenue of income to support you. This is also why I mentioned having other means of adult oriented product's income, as well as affiliate marketing sales. I hope this chapter gave you a clearer description of what WRITER'S BLOCK is all about.

Even as I write this there have been times, I had to step away to gather my thoughts in context, to write as much about this, as I possibly could. I wanted you to have the wealth of my knowledge, even though to some it might seem limited. The one good thing about Writer's Block, is its complete opposite. That is when the writing creative thoughts flow through your head even faster than you can write them down. This is what I call being in THE ZONE.

I know I have gone back to read many of my older works of erotica, only to find myself wondering, who the hell wrote this. I was often astonished at how really in THE ZONE that some were, while others could always use a little rewriting.

That is the thing about writing. You write, rewrite, and rewrite again, and then you edit it, and rewrite again until you finish. Word to the wise, like with any artist, do not overwork your work. An artist needs to sign the painting, so that it can be exhibited and sold.

Chapter 32: Pseudonyms

Guess what? These never change either. Now I have seen some new publications online listing dirty words. I have checked some out. Sometimes I feel it is best to just use a word, and then look it up, which is researching, in a hard copy, or digital, thesaurus.

Chapter 33: Payment

Payment has not changed much unless you like bitcoin. Many offer payment by PayPal, direct deposit to your bank accounts, and check. So, this chapter we will leave alone. What has changed is the various ways you can make additional income with your erotica. Have you been to my website yet? bbpierceauthor.com[1]

You will see I sell my erotica from there and have other pages for selling adult-oriented products, affiliate marketing (which is referring customers to another website and receiving a portion of the profits from their sale), plus trade web links with other erotica authors. I even have a link to my other products that I design and sell, which have an adult oriented design. Further in this book I cover Affiliate Marketing.

Many of you still might just want to write erotica, and not sell it. Perhaps you only want to write a few to submit to websites that do not pay, only to get feedback from them. This is entirely up to you.

So, your erotica writing does not have to be the one way you can earn money from it. You must be creative in other ways you can make money in the adult industry because there are plenty of them. Please take a moment and visit my website. BTW any of you with an erotica writer, or adult oriented product website, please contact me if you would like to trade web links with me. bbpierceauthor@yahoo.com

---

1. http://bbpierceauthor.com

Chapter 34: Sample Letters & Submission Logs

Sample letters, and submission logs can still be used. I do not use them anymore, simply because I do not submit my work as I used to. Now, I simply self-publish it. Then each self-published book/story has a folder. Those folders are in a finished self-published book folder for Amazon. Now, once I start to branch out with self-publishing to other platforms I will create similar files, and folders for them.

I am not using paper as before, because everything is stored on my MacBook. Look at the bright side, no paper saves Forests.

However, if this is the avenue you wish to follow, then do so. If you do, then everything in the original edition will be what you need to follow.

Chapter 35: Sexciting Words That Sizzle

At this point I do not think you need more of my dirty words. Once you begin writing and using the ones in the beginning of the book, I am quite sure that you will begin thinking of your own to use. Trust me, I have faith in your dirty minds.

In the hopes of helping other authors, there is at least one book I know of that has lists of Dirty Words. You can find it online.

OK, here is just one more to get you thinking dirty, not that most of you need any encouragement in this area. Otherwise, you would not be writing erotica, or beginning to learn how too.

goop

Chapter 36: Greeting Cards and Adult Oriented Humor

Obviously, the greeting card industry is not what it used to be considering email and texting. I do have other ways you can make money with humor, and adult humor. Plus, this is yet one other area for you to research. Have you ever thought of comedy writing?

The adult greeting card companies are still out there. I have begun another venue entirely, graphic design. It is POD print on demand, and the designs can be printed on just about anything, even bumper stickers, stickers, and magnets. You decide what you want to market your adult humor on. My website is. casualteesoffashion.com[1] I have all sorts of graphic designs, and various albums, or collections. One being Adults Only, and many are extremely sexually graphic.

The beauty is that they can be printed on just about anything. So, if you do not have the balls to wear it as attire on the street, you can still drink from a coif mug with the design, or maybe just a refrigerator magnet? Did I mention there is an album/collection just for Writers? I invite you to visit the website. Normally there are monthly up to 35-40% off sales, so be sure to bookmark the website.

Here are a few adult oriented humor greeting card websites. There are many more, which are humorous, just not adult oriented. If you wish to research these, I highly suggest that you do so.

zazzle.com[2]
alwaysfits.com[3]
nobleworkscards.com[4]
cafepress.com[5]

---

1.   http://casualteesoffashion.com

2.   http://zazzle.com

3.   http://alwaysfits.com

4.   http://nobleworkscards.com

5.   http://cafepress.com

untamedego.com[6]

---

6.   http://untamedego.com

Chapter 37: Over 250 Story Line ideas

OK, I will list a few more for you, however you have so damn many now. It is up to you, and your very dirty mind to COME UP with more of them to write about.

1. This is a great one. Take your entire day. Let's say you have a job. So, take the entire day from the time you awake to time you go to bed. Think of all the scenarios you are experiencing. You got this. I am just going to list quick subject matter here: Any sex you had, spy on cheating neighbors, drive to work nude in car, truckers watching, wondering about hot drivers/passengers in other cars, or you take public transportation, this gets even better, at work colleagues you had sex with or who are having sex with each other or even cheating, a business luncheon at a local hotel restaurant, a hotel filled with endless bedrooms for endless sex, waiters/waitresses flirting with you, Imagining your luncheon companion and their sexual appetites or if they are well hung or not, or shaved or unshaved straight/ bisexual/gay, again back at office ideas, drive or ride home ideas, at home delivery people stopping by, mail carriers, again spying on kinky neighbors, or maybe it is you putting on a kinky show for them, then you shower and go to bed, & your sexual activities whether alone or with someone? See all these storyline scenarios just from your personal life, you can only imagine how many other that you can COME UP with, without my help now. So go for it.

1. Sit at the mall food courts and study the people, take notes for character studies, also a mall scenario for an erotica story.

Salesclerks, shoe sale people, dressing room sex. Caught shop lifting by security and what you must do to be released without being charged.

3. Movie theaters and concerts

4. Doctor/dentist visits

5. Any and all the kinky sex habits you can think of, or fantasize about

6. Covid-19 quarantining

7. High school reunions old flames, and those you never had the opportunity of being with before

8. An unscrupulous landlord, and how the rent gets paid, being spied on, missing panties, caught masturbating when you thought you were alone

9. The life of a Sissy and how it all CAME about for them

10. Age gap romance of all kinds, ages, shapes sizes, races, and couple sexes

11. Research an entirely new kink that you never wrote about and then research that niche to see if it is worth writing about as far as sale popularity. If it is worth writing about, then write about it.

12. Have you ever considered your own deep dark kinky fetish sexual fantasies yet? If so great, way to go. If not and you find they are sellable as far as what erotica readers want, then write about them.

13. Your car breaks down in front of a nudist colony late one dark and stormy rainy night.

14. You tag along with some gay friends to a gay bar, and once there get bold and decide to test the waters for the very first time.

15. You run into your babysitter years later when you are over eighteen years of age.

16. Seduced by an in-law. Maybe you seduce and in-law?

17. You have a fetish for chubby women or men, and your chubby chasing escapade experiences.

18. You finally save up enough money to purchase a high end almost real looking silicone sex doll and what life is like having sex with it.

19. Your very first 18+ sexual experience.

20. You have a fetish for tiny dick men and what you experience having sex with them.

21. You are a gay male with a fetish for dirty dicks, especially uncircumcised ones with man skank under the folds of foreskin.

22. As a real estate sales associate or broker just what it takes to close a deal, or maybe you sell cars and what happened in an SUV in the very last lane on the sales lot one night before making the sale

23. What happens in an adult movie theatre in there dark while the movie plays, this may have to be a period piece due to them not having those types of theaters around today

24. What goes on behind the scenes of filming an adult video between the crew members and maybe even the cast & talent

25. Answering a classified ad for being wanted to be spanked subject to BDSM, tickled, humiliated, exhibited naked to the public etc.

26. Stripped naked and brought to a seedier part of town and dropped off to roam for a set period before being picked up safely or within your own suburban neighborhood where someone might recognize you.

27. A large condo or apartment complex in city where you can see into many neighbor's windows, and they can see into yours and just what you see or what others see you do.

28. First time fisting. Solo, MM, MF, FF.

29. Getting or giving a lap dance in private VIP area of strip club.

30. In a university, college, junior city college, and what you do or allow to be done to you for a passing grade.

31. Just a reminder here, many of these storyline ideas, if not all of them, can be MF, FF, MM. MFM, FMF, and/or solo scenarios. This greatly increases your number of stories that you can create.

32. Making additional income being a sex toy reviewer and your personal experiences either alone or with others.

33. Making additional income selling well-worn dirty panties.

34. Making additional income with feet photos and sale of worn shoes and socks.

35. Making additional income making amateur adult videos to sell.

36. Making additional income shooting nudes and nude selfies and what you are doing while shooting. Perhaps having sex with your photographer. Maybe you are the photographer shooting the nudes.

37. A reverse of the above 5, you are being the customers for them and what you do with them and/or request to the content providers.

38. First time anal. Solo, MM, MF, FF, FM.

39. Being an exhibitionist. Flashing others in car, in city, streaking, etc.

40. Adult baby fetish role play.

41. Role play in general. Characters, scenarios, diaper, Daddy, Mommy, Sissy, Spanking punishment, etc.

42. BDSM tickling.

43. Sex on a boat, luxury cruise line vacation, singles, or swinger cruise.

44. Begging for a pegging? Submissive, first timers, repeat offenders.

45. Working in a sex toy manufacturing plant, or as a sales rep.

46. Sex therapist

47. Youngest male at a senior citizen retreat community and servicing all the ladies

48. Representative for sex doll company and sell to senior men in retirement center

49. Employee at adult sex toy video shop arcade

50. 21-year-old new employee at a swinger club

51. YOU do the math 250 + 50 = 300 Storyline Ideas. So never tell me you do not have any erotic story ideas. Plus, from these you should be able to create even more to write about.

Chapter 38: Adult Publishers' Addresses

Yes, many are still out there, again another item to research. What you need to do now is research the websites out there. Yes, not to worry, I will list some in here for you. It is just now with all the websites you must do some research as well. There is also the hard copy of The Writer's Market, however they do not list many adult publications, unfortunately.

What I do is Google "erotica publishers" and see what pops up. I suggest you also do the same and a few variations as well. You can do the same with romance, since some rom once publishers will also accept erotica. You just must find which ones they are. Some of these might be just erotic romance publishers for those of you still uncertain of just how hard core and kinky erotica you want to write.

Again, I urge you to do your own erotica publishers research since many of these links may no longer be active. Plus, always be aware of non-secure pages http is not secure https is secure. So be careful when opening non secure sites. Unfortunately, there are still websites that do not feel they need to pay the additional fees for security. So always do your due diligence. These are purposely not hyperlinked so as not to conflict any interests of my self-publishing websites.

kdp.amazon.com

lethepressbooks.com

press.barnesandnoble.com

pinkflamingo.com

cleispress.com

smashwords.com

medium.com

apple.com/apple-books/

sirenbookstrand.com

blurb.com

draft2digital.com

lulu.com

blackvelvetseductions.com

imajinnbooks.com

jms-books.com

smutpire.com

12.eroticpleasurespublishing.com

decadentpublishing.com

romance.ink.com

circlet.com

martianmigrainepress.com

dreamspinnerpress.com

totallybound.com

bellabooks.com

blackvelvetseductions.com

boldstrokesbooks.com

boroughspublishinggroup.com

changelingpress.com

bookouture.com

desertpalmpress.com

flashpointpublications.com

hugedomains.com

koreropress.com

mélange-books.com

peaceinthestormpublishing.com

eroticbooknetwork.com

redsagepub.com

riptidepublishing.com

simonandschuster.com

smutpire.com

supposedcrimes.com

tenthstreetpress.com

eroticpleasurespublishing.com

pegasuspublishers.com
penguinrandomhouse.com
austinmacauley.com
authorspublish.com
reddit.com
whizbuzzbooks.com

Chapter 39: Pen Pal Groups

As for these I have researched a few yet leave this up to you. Not many are as pen pal oriented now, especially with all the forums, chat rooms, groups, etc. online these days. So please do your due diligence here. Below you will find several I have researched or googled for you. Please bear in mind that I am not saying any of these are worthwhile. I just googled "erotica pen pal groups" and these popped up. Always do your own due diligence.

https://lovehoneyforum.com/t/erotic-penpals/230417
https://erotic-penpals.livejournal.com
https://alt.penpals.forty-plus-yrs.narkive.com/zJljLqew/erotic-penpals-unite

Chapter 40: Websites Pertaining to Writing Erotica & Stories

These come into play now, even more importantly than before, simply because there are so many of them. It will be up to you to select the ones that serve you the most. This is all governed by the kinky niche that you write erotica about. Remember I used to review amateur adult videos, and some pro erotica videos as well, so you might also find some to write about. There are plenty of adult websites that may need reviewing since so many keep popping up.

Maybe you could offer your personal erotica expertise services to others? Meanwhile, here are a few that have all sorts of erotica stories that should wet your erotica writing appetites even more.

https://www.lushstories.com
https://noveltrove.com
https://bdsmcafe.com
https://www.solotouch.com/#gsc.tab=0[1]
http://www.bdsmlibrary.com
https://juicysexstories.com
https://fictionmania.tv
https://www.literotica.com
https://chyoa.com
https://eroticastory.ca
https://fictionmania.tv
https://j-bays.com/php/index.php
https://contoeroticoprive.com
https://www.asstr.org/main.html

Chapter 41: Marketing Using Social Media

Social media is BIG. As for myself I use Facebook, Twitter, Instagram Pinterest, not to mention having my own websites. So, I invite you to LIKE me, FOLLOW me, and post your comments to my pages bbpierceauthor

Unfortunately, it is time consuming, yet as an author you need to market your work. Yes, you can research and find others willing to do it for you for a fee. There is software you can purchase that will help save you time and effort, although you must pay for it. This just depends how much money you must put into your writing. Normally beginner writers are not so fortunate to have much money to spend on their writing. So, if you do, then great, go for it.

Once you have your social media accounts set up you can begin promoting your work. I suggest you also spend time on them engaging with others, so they get to know you. Do not just promote your work and nothing else. Be helpful to others where and when you can. I make it a point to promote other authors whenever I can. Since I have been doing this awhile, I also offer my help to anyone just beginning to write erotica, thus this book for instance.

I have had the pleasure to meet many other writers online and have benefited from them as well as helped them. Facebook has several GROUPS for erotica and writers. Some are for helping one another and many are simply for self-promotion. So again, I suggest you research them all. If social media is a bit challenging for you, you might want to read some self-help books about them. Amazon Kindle Unlimited has many, and if you are a member, you can read them for FREE. I am a member and get my monies worth many times over for what I spend for the fee. Plus, you must realize once you begin making money as an erotica writer, then you can deduct many of these necessary expenses on your taxes.

Be sure to like and share what others post and reply to them, retweet them, ping them, depending on what social media platform you are on at the time. Research each one, because each are different. Many allow you to have several accounts. So, you can have a personal one, and one for your pen name.

The is also paid advertising available on most social media accounts, as well as Amazon itself, if you choose to self-publish with Amazon Kindle. This is just one of the websites where I currently self-publish.

Now there are some websites that will promote your work for free. Then there are many in the business of doing just that, promoting your books for a fee. I highly suggest you get reviews and speak with others who use them. This way you have a good idea of what you can expect from them.

Another form of promotion is book reviews and ratings. Amazon has a rating at the end of each eBook. I always ask for reviews, because as many of you know I am quite anal bout this. I always say if you read an erotica book, then review it. Authors always like to read reviews of their work, good or bad, well at least I do. This way I can become a better writer. I listen to what my readers have to say about my writing, what they like and/or dislike about my stories. In a way this allows the erotica readers to partake in erotica writing, whether they realize it or not.

Many erotica readers do not like to leave reviews because they will be in their real names. This I highly understand and have come up with a solution. I ask all my readers to dm, message me, or email me bbpierceauthor@yahoo.com, and to use the word anonymous since it is only me seeing who they are when they email me. Then I use their anonymous reviews on my social media posts, in my upcoming books, my website, etc. I also suggest they state they state and/or country that they reside in. This way they get to review my work, and I get a review to use in the future. A win-win for everyone.

Chapter 42: Designing Your Own Book Covers

Designing book covers is fun for me, however I have an art background. I am an artist's, photographer, and videographer, which helps immensely. I will only be speaking about using Canva Pro, canva.com[1] although there is a limited free version of it that you can try. The pro edition just gives you more to work with as far as photos, templates, etc. Bear in mind I am also an affiliate marketer for Canva.

Canva offer photos to use, which I do use some of theirs. There are many other stock photo websites to choose from, online. Again, I suggest that you do research on this. One I also use is Pixabay, pixabay.com[2] which I do pay a yearly subscription fee to. It also provides vectors that I use for graphic designs. Now I read lots of other erotica writer's books and have read where one does not recommend Pixabay.

Bear in mind I am not recommending any of the links, products, software etc. that I mention in this book. I am simply showing you, my process. It is always up to you, to research and review all of it before making your final decisions. I can always change my mind as well. There are many other websites and software.

Many of the lists I have compiled in the revised section could have a few not be available right after I included them, while new ones might pop up and I will have missed them. So, it is always best to check researched references on a regular basis to make sure you have the most up to date information at hand.

Besides book covers, I also use Canva Pro for all my social media post designs, as well as other designs. Check out their website, and see for yourself, just how many different types of design templates that they have to offer. So, you can see the importance of Canva Pro for me.

1. http://canva.com

2.   http://pixabay.com

There are just so many ways that you can use it. Bear in mind there are several other websites just like it, although for these you will have to do your research.

Now eBooks are one size book cover, while paperbacks are another. I have yet to design any book covers for paperbacks, however I plan too soon.

Online through social media pages I also offer advice and free help by answering questions for anyone wanting to know more about designing book covers using Canva. So, if any of you have any questions, please contact me vis Dm, Message, or email bbpierceauthor@yahoo.com

You can also research to find artists who will create book covers for you, for a fee. fiverr.com[3] is one of those websites. You can post your need/request for a book cover designer on social media and see who responds. Again, I suggest you get accurate reviews of them first before making your choices. Contact me with any questions.

https://getcovers.com

---

3.   http://fiverr.com

Chapter 43: The Importance of Having a Website

I have several websites, the one for my erotica writing is,

bbpierceauthor (dot) com

Websites are important for branding yourself as a writer. You can have one for each of your pen names. I send those that visit my site to my author's pages for purchasing my books. I have other pages pertaining to other adult oriented products and vendors. We trade web links with others, plus have affiliate marketing adult oriented as well as writing products for sale. So, a website can bring you revenue from all angles. It just depends how creative and diverse you want to be.

You can also have other websites which you can send customers to, or you can send them to this one from another.

BTW I also created my own website with godaddy.com[1]

For those who would not be able to do your own websites, GoDaddy has services for you, not to mention all other types of website designers and other companies able to host your domain. I am merely letting you know the avenues I have taken to get to this point in my career. There are many domain hosts to research.

Another plus of having a website is that you can offer a FREE newsletter to subscribers, which also gives you their emails, plus each month you can send them a newsletter, promoting your latest books, and anything else you feel they would be interested in. You can even mention upcoming books and anything else that you might be affiliate marketing at the time. This is how you accumulate email lists also.

---

1.   http://godaddy.com

Chapter 44: Writing Software and Writing Tools

Any of the products that you find listed here I am not saying that they are the best. I am merely showing you some that are available Again, this is an area you need to research. Anything that I am an affiliate marketer for I will mention it because I would receive a slight compensation should you purchase it with my id link. I find it is always best to research products by reading reviews others have written about them. Just make sure these are independent reviews, and not reviews of the product by the company that manufacturers them.

To begin with I will simply mention potential ones, and then I will list links to them for you to gather more information.

There is software for eBook formatting, word processing, graphic designs, keyword search, audio dictation, grammar, domain/website hosting, and much much more. Then you have actual products, such as computers, keyboards, photography, and video equipment. For me to make long lists here would not be time worthy. Instead, I suggest you research and review these products and websites on your own. Now should some of this be too taxing for you, in the event it is completely new to you, then indeed, contact me with any questions. Hopefully, I can direct you to where you best need to go for the answers that you are seeking.

Adobe designs can be used for book covers.

Recording, then having dictating software write it, or you can just dictate to the software.

Pocket rocket is great for finding proper keywords.

Canva can be used to make book covers and social media posts.

Chapter 45: Pen Names

Having a pen name for writing erotica is imperative, unless you want the entire world to know you write erotica. The beauty of a pen name for writing, is that you can have as many as you wish. You can write with a male, or female pen name. Plus, you can use initials, so readers do not know what sex you are. Take mine for instance, B. B. Pierce. What does B. B. stand for?

Chapter 46: Formatting for Self-Publishing & Audio Books

I so far have only formatted for Amazon, and only for eBooks. Paperbacks I have yet to format, however I plan to in the very near future, with a paperback version of this book. Also, I plan to step away from Kindle Select, and self-publish on other platforms. I too will have to learn this new form of formatting, which is different from Amazon. You may not wish to self-publish on Amazon and go directly to a different self-publishing platform. Currently, I can only explain the Amazon Kindle self-publishing platform. My website BLOG will have updates.

As for audio books, this again is an area I have yet to format for, however will do in the future. So, for audio formatting, I suggest you research it further, as it is something I am not experienced with. However, I do plan to venture into it soon. I know that there are professionals you can hire to read your work. You might consider reading it yourself, depending on your voice and reading skills.

Now let me get back to the task at hand formatting for Amazon eBooks. No matter what format you created your story/book in you can export it to word or pub it. I write with Pages and export to word. Once you have your word/dox or pub, then it is time to use Kindle Create.

What I do is to write down all the pertinent information I will need, so that when it is needed, all I must do is copy and paste it. Some of the material you almost never need to change, while others must change for each new eBook self-publication. This is part of the importance of keeping writing folder/files. You will also need to have a jpg of your eBook cover design handy, and for when you begin the KDP process.

So, once you have all the necessary pages, and designs, then you are ready to begin with Kindle Create. This is the list of pages they offer you to include in your book. You can use them all, or just the ones that you choose to use.

Title Page
Epigraph
Dedication
Description
Copyright
Preface
Introduction
Prologue
Forward
Table Of Contents
Epilogue
Author Bio
Author Book List
Afterward

Once you are finished with Kindle Create, then you are ready to proceed to the Kindle Direct Publishing page, which will bring you through a further process.

I must mention that I have only self-published with Amazon Kindle Unlimited in eBook format. I next plan on a few paperbacks to self-publish. Then I plan to research other self-publishing websites. I understand they use other formatting so be prepared to learn other formatting structures. Many may not require as much as Amazon Kindle does, and some may require more.

Chapter 47: Affiliate Marketing

What is affiliate marketing, you may ask?

Affiliate marketing is a type of performance-based marketing in which a business rewards one or more affiliates for each visitor or customer brought by the affiliate's own marketing efforts. Wikipedia[1]

The beauty of it is that it allows you to make additional income by just becoming an affiliate marketer for a company and/or product, and then posting links throughout social media and your website. You can even link them from your writing within your books, if they should apply to them.

For instance, you write erotica and perhaps can link to adult oriented products should they fit into your story or book. I link most of mine from my website and my blogs. At times, I do link from my social media accounts.

With Amazon you can also sign up so you can obtain affiliate marketing for individual products. This way you can only use specific products that might apply to a specific story, blog, or book.

Again, I ask you to research this, since this book is about writing erotica and not affiliate marketing. I am merely mentioning it so you can see, yet another way to increase your additional income potential from your own erotic writing. Visit my website and check out my resource pages there. Each is devoted to a particular adult oriented subject matter and/or product. Some have affiliates, while others simply have web links. Trading website links is a great free way to broaden your potential customer reach. I am always open to trade adult-oriented website links.

1.   https://en.wikipedia.org/wiki/Affiliate_marketing

Chapter 48: Facebook Groups to Join for Erotica Writers & Readers

Books Of an Adult Nature
    Writers Club
    Erotic & Kinky Book Promotion
    Nina's Friendly Erotic Adult Book Club
    Writer To Writer
    The Writers Forum
    Erotica Is Not Porn Promo and Review Swap
    ROSE (Romance of Sensual Erotica)
    Booties Book Promo Group
    Taboo and Kinky Reads
    Erotica, Sex, and Sin
    Erotica Authors Unite!
    Erotica Reads Promotion Group
    Erotica Readers and Authors
    No Limits Pimping
    All Books - All Genres
    The New Writers and Authors
    Erotic Erotica Authors Promo Group
    Writers and Authors Promotions
    Erotica
    Kindle & eBooks For Authors and Readers
    Leeny's Lovers Erotica Group
    Self-Publishing Support Group
    Erotica For 18+
    <Kindle eBook Promotion> Authors, Writers, and Bloggers
    Creative Writing
    Naked Friday Party and Books

A Quietstorm Erotica Book Promotions

For The Love of Books Promo Groups

Kindle Authors and Readers

Writers, Beta Readers, Critique, Advice, Writing Exercises & ....

Writers Authors and Readers

Writers Helping Writers

The write place.

Kindle Unlimited - FREE READS and Subscribers

Kindle Book Club - authors & readers

New Writers and Authors

Book Review & Promotion

Club Romance Book Bar

Free Book Promotion!

Daniella Story Palace

Books, Blogs, Readers, Writers, and Promoters

The Book Stop: Authors & Readers Welcome

Aspiring Writers United

eBook

Rockin Book Divas

Taboo Erotica Readers and Writers

Book Promotions

Love 2 read Romance, Erotica, BDSM

Indie Author's eBook and Paperback Promotion

Andreas All Things Promotion

Book Promotions

Books With 20 Reviews or Less Promotions

Book Pixie Promo

English Writers

Mynae's Book Nook

Adventures Unlimited Books

Kindle readers and authors

Independent Authors

Only Free Kindle Books
Writers and Readers Unite
Independent Authors Book Promotion
Books with warning labels.
For Writers, By Authors
Underrated Writers/Readers
The Book HQ
Authors Share Your Posts
Fiction Lovers Forum! Find Greta Books Here!!
Book Love and Promotions
Short Fiction Writers and Readers
Rylee's Kindle Book Promo's
Book Promotions!!!
Authors and Writers Promotions
Authors Promoting Authors

I suggest you create a Facebook page for your author pen name. This allows you to promote yourself there plus you can then join the groups which pertain to your writing. Many will allow you to promote your work and it is a good place to find erotica readers.

Chapter 49: Why We Write Erotica

I know why I write erotica, I have a DIRTY MIND, and perhaps an overly active sexual imagination. Why do you write erotica, or want to write erotica? You must know the answer to this question. I wish I could write about other subjects as easily as I can write erotica. Sadly, I cannot, so I write erotica instead. I suppose if I could write about other subjects as easily as erotica COMES to me, I would be dangerous.

If you enjoy writing erotica, and are compassionate about it, then write it, and keep writing it. Again, anyone reading this who has any questions for me about erotica writing, please contact me with these questions. Dm, message, or email me. **bbpierceauthor@yahoo.com**

Chapter 50: Closing Thoughts

As I COME to a close with this book revision, I want to thank all of you readers for taking the time to purchase and read this book about How To write erotica. I hope it helps you and answers all your questions so that you can continue to write erotica, or start in the event you are a newbie, or a wanna be erotica writer. Never be ashamed of writing erotica, I certainly am not. You are a writer, an artist honing your craft.

Many of you will find that you could crossover to romance fiction, while many may even be able to write mainstream fiction, or nonfiction.

Good luck with your writing adventure. Start writing, and keep writing, and stay safe. Write and read erotica responsibly.

Most important, when you read erotica, or any subject matter book, please review/rate it for the author. Reviews help authors to become that much better. Plus, in erotica, I always ask my readers what kinky niches they want me to write more stories about, or maybe even something completely new for them. This is a win-win for everyone. The last chapter has some resources, and a list of my current eBooks, this one being also my first paperback, due to the length, although I plan on self-publishing a few of my other lengthier eBooks into paperbacks.

Readers, in closing, thank you for reading me, please review/rate me, and stay safe.

Chapter 51: Resources & List of B. B. Pierce Erotica

These are just a few last-minute website links that I found while researching this revision. So, take them at your leisure, some may be of interest to you, and some may not. I just thought that they were amicable for your reads and thoughts, whether they are of interest and use to you, as an erotica writer. Remember, there are many many more of these on the internet, so do YOUR due diligence and research as many as possible.

https://www.erotica-readers.com[1]
    https://www.facebook.com/eroticareadersandwriters/
    http://eroticauthorsguild.org

---

1. https://www.erotica-readers.com

Chapter 52: Author's Notes

I hope all of you received something from reading this book. Thank all of you so much for your loyalty, as readers of B. B. Pierce.

Many of you already write erotica, and most likely read this book seeking anything you could utilize to further your erotica writing. On the same note, many of you read this book because you are considering becoming an erotica writer. Regardless of your reasons, I want all of you to know that I am always here for you should you have questions. Contact me via DM, or message on any of my social media platforms. Email me at bbpierceauthor@yahoo.com. My website bbpierceauthor (dot) com offers you a free e-newsletter. If any of you have an erotica writer website, I invite you to trade web links with me. This also goes for anyone offering adult content on the internet, or any adult product manufacturers who are looking for affiliate marketers.

So now it is all up to you entirely. Begin now to write erotica if you are thinking about it. If you already write erotica, continue your erotica writing. The erotica writing world is your oyster, so start shucking.

Again, I humbly thank all of you, and wish you all the best of luck with your erotica writing endeavors. Keep writing erotica, keep selling it, and stay safe.

"A DIRTY MIND is a terrible thing to waste, especially YOURS."

Connect With Author B.B. Pierce

always ask my readers to review my eBooks/Books after reading them.
will never use your real name just the word, anonymous, unless you
ell me to use your real name or initials. DM me at any of my social
media pages or email me at bbpierceauthor@yahoo.com

I am on Facebook, and Twitter as @BBPierce2, or bbpierceauthor
o just search for me. Please FOLLOW & LIKE

My website is bbpierceauthor (dot) com the word "dot" meaning.

I purposely did not list it as a hyperlink because it has links to other
vendor websites, which can be a conflict of interest to some.

My website also has a wide variety of Adult Content available to
ou. Many links to all kinds of kinks, plus links to other erotica authors.
Adult oriented attire, feet pix and custom videos, shoes, panties,
magazines, newsletters, sex toys, sex dolls, and blogs. Even a link to
freelance jobs in the adult industry.

Send for my FREE Erotica E-newsletter.

More erotica eBooks/Books can be found on most online eBook/Book
ales platforms.

Stay safe.

Read erotica responsibly.

Books by BB Pierce.

Please visit your favorite online eBook/Book retailer to discover othe books by

B. B. Pierce

Writing Erotica for Fun & Profit Revised Edition: Beginner WelCOME. "Learn How to Improve your creative writing process s you can write sexually graphic, dirty, kinky, nasty erotic stories. 30 FREE erotica story ideas included so YOU can begin writing erotic immediately. Plus, FREE Q&A with me and I will review one of you first drafts if you wish."

An Older Woman: Found Out About My Foot Fetish: "Foot fetis kinks"

Red Satin Sheets: An Older Woman and A Younger Man: "Ag Gap Sex"

Sexy Horny Nasty Dirty Kinky MILFS Volume One: "Ever bee seduced by an older woman? Or been willingly submissive to dominant Cougar?"

Sexy Horny Dirty Nasty Kinky MILFS Volume Two: "Did on of your friends Moms ever hit on you? Did you fantasize about he sexually?"

Sexy Horny Dirty Nasty Kinky MILFS Volume Three: "Some offe sexual services while others sell worn soiled smelly panties, and man just love other women."

Sexy Horny Dirty Nasty Kinky MILFS Volume Four: "Olde horny females can be kinky beyond belief. Age gap sex."

Sexy Horny Dirty Nasty Kinky MILFs. Volume. Five: "Olde females are hot and horny especially for much younger men."

Sexy Horny Dirty Nasty Kinky MILFs. Volume. Six: "Would yo enjoy being spanked by an older woman? Perhaps you already have."

Panty Lover's Paradise Volume One: "Ever stollen dirty pantie from the laundry room in your building? Did you ever want to?"

Panty Lover's Paradise Volume Two: "A Must-Read Panty Fetish Erotica for Those Who Smell Sniff Sell Wear and/or Worship Dirty Worn Used Female Panties"

Panty Lover's Paradise Volume Three: "What about dirty hamper diving at your friend's home and finding his wife's dirty cum stained panties?"

Panty Lover's Paradise Volume Four: "Ever wear a pair to work or had a GF make you wear hers while she watched you masturbate in them for her?"

Granny Panties and Foot Massages: "I love the smell of arthritic cream."

Smell My Feet Volume One: "Stinky Sweaty Smelly Dirty Dainty Foot Fetishes"

Smell My Feet Volume Two: "Foot jobs galore and stank female feet odors to die for."

Smell My Feet Volume Three: Stinky Sweaty Smelly Dirty Dainty Foot Fetishes "Do you like wearing high heels in private and worshipping bare feet?"

Nasty Dirty Stinky Sweaty Smelly Female Foot Fetish EROTICA "Hot foot fetish and worshipping erotica"

Sexy Sissy Panties: Volume One: "Sissyfication feminization sissygasms"

The SISSY and the DOCTOR Volume One: "Sissygasms galore panty fetish foot fetish anal and oral exploration and latex gloved role play."

The Sissy and The Doctor Volume Two: "Bizarre orgies LGBTQ age gap BDSM sex man of the house issues brat situations spankings size humiliation menage couplings."

The Art of Feminization: How Bradley BeCAME Brandy "Detailed evolution of a young sissy to feminization spanking oral and anal sex"

Lez Be Friends: 5 Lesbian Loving Stories of Old and Younger Firs
Timers Gym Shower Military Kinky and More "So many lick he
problem solutions."

A Lesbian Story: A Woman's Wet Kiss "Lesbian lewd lust firs
time."

An LGBT Story Women Loving Women "Hot kinky stinky female
sex"

A Lusty Librarian: A Lesbian in An All-Female College "She i
insatiable. This is a long read."

Gay Sex Bisexual College Roommates: Graphic Sexual Story o
Seduction and Submission "His first time straight bisexual LGBTQ
anal spanking and oral sex."

Bound For Glory Holes: Gay Bisexual Men's Shameful Lewd
Sexual Desires in Adult Bookstore Video Arcades and Elsewhere
"Straight male first time gay & becomes addicted. His actions inside
the tiny booth are downright disgusting."

An Older Woman the College Nurse: And Her Kinky Medica
Examinations

"Age gap invasion of a younger innocent male with medica
procedures."

Hot Hairy Horny Dirty Nasty Women: Unshaven Fuzzy Curly
Kinky Bushy Matted Unshorn Briskly Bush Stubbly Erotica "For those
with hair fetishes."

Hot Hairy Horny Dirty Nasty Women. Volume Two: Unshaver
Fuzzy Curly Kinky Bushy Matted Unshorn Briskly Bush Stubbly
"Hairy female fetishes, many of which may shock you."

Femdom Erotica: Domination Station Volume One "Female
dominates several other females and maybe at least one mos
unfortunate male."

The Commander: The Maledom of Katherine "A big kinky
dominator of beautiful trophy wives, all paid for by their unsuspecting
husbands."

The Knotty Naughty Sailor: Submissive Female Tied Bound Restrained Tickled Spanked to Multiple Orgasms & More "BDSM erotica adventures of a young couple meeting for the first time at an alternative lifestyle establishment."

MILF: 20 Assorted Older Women Younger Men Sexxxual Climaxing Stories

"Got MILF? Yes, we do ass much age gap role play erotica ass you can read."

Taboo Erotica MILF: Volume One "His stepmom is horny and afraid."

MILF Taboo: Volume Two "His stepmom has some hot kinky friends for him."

I Was Caught by An Older Woman: Spanking Humiliation Sexual Redemption Age Gap Erotica "Age gap sex a male virgin comes of age masturbation horror and perverted older female administered sexual punishment you cannot believe."

Erotica You Need to Read: A Sexxxy Assortment of Kinky Fetishes to Choose From "All sorts of kinky depraved erotica imaginable inside and more."

Nasty Kinky Dirty Step Daddy Desires: Taboo Erotica "Role play age gap. Man of the house with a brat. First time anal oral sexual scenarios and more."

Daddy's Big Girl Older Men and Much Younger Women Naughty Sexy Kinky Dirty Little Teasers: Taboo Erotica "Age gap man of house role play sex. Watching porn first time together with anal and oral orgasming."

My Sissy Niece: Taboo Erotica "Young male to female age gap role play sex after feminization. Kinkiness hardcore sex spanking anal oral menage with dirty talk."

Consider yourself invited to my website!

Again, I will not use the hyperlink as it is controversial for many vendors. Please be sure to bookmark it though. bbpierceauthor (dot) com. Now you know (dot) means a period. .

If you are not completely spent, I suggest you go to it now. I have all sorts of kinky lewd decadent Adult Oriented things there waiting just for you. Worn panties, worn shoes, feet pix, custom amateur adult videos, adult oriented attire, sex toys, sex dolls, links to other erotica authors, magazines, newsletters, blogs, even freelance adult industry jobs, and much more.

Sign up for my FREE E-newsletter.

Stay safe, happy, healthy, and most important HORNY.

I thank you for reading my erotica and hope you enjoyed it. Please send me a review so I can use it on my website homepage and on my social media posts and tweets.

B. B. Pierce

Ingram Content Group UK Ltd.
Milton Keynes UK
UKHW010636050623
422889UK00001B/191